THE WORLD OF BLANTYRE

CLAIRE HOPLEY

& THE COOKERY OF CHRISTOPHER BROOKS

We welcome your comments and suggestions.
Please contact:

Blantyre
P.O. Box 995; 16 Blantyre Road
Lenox MA 01240
(413) 637-3556
E-Mail: bookone@blantyre.com

ISBN: 978-0-615-25678-8

Book design by Rita Marshall
Printed by Excelsior Printing Company

Published by Blantyre, P.O. Box 995, Lenox MA 01240

First Printing

Vichyssoise recipe appears on page 178

Contents

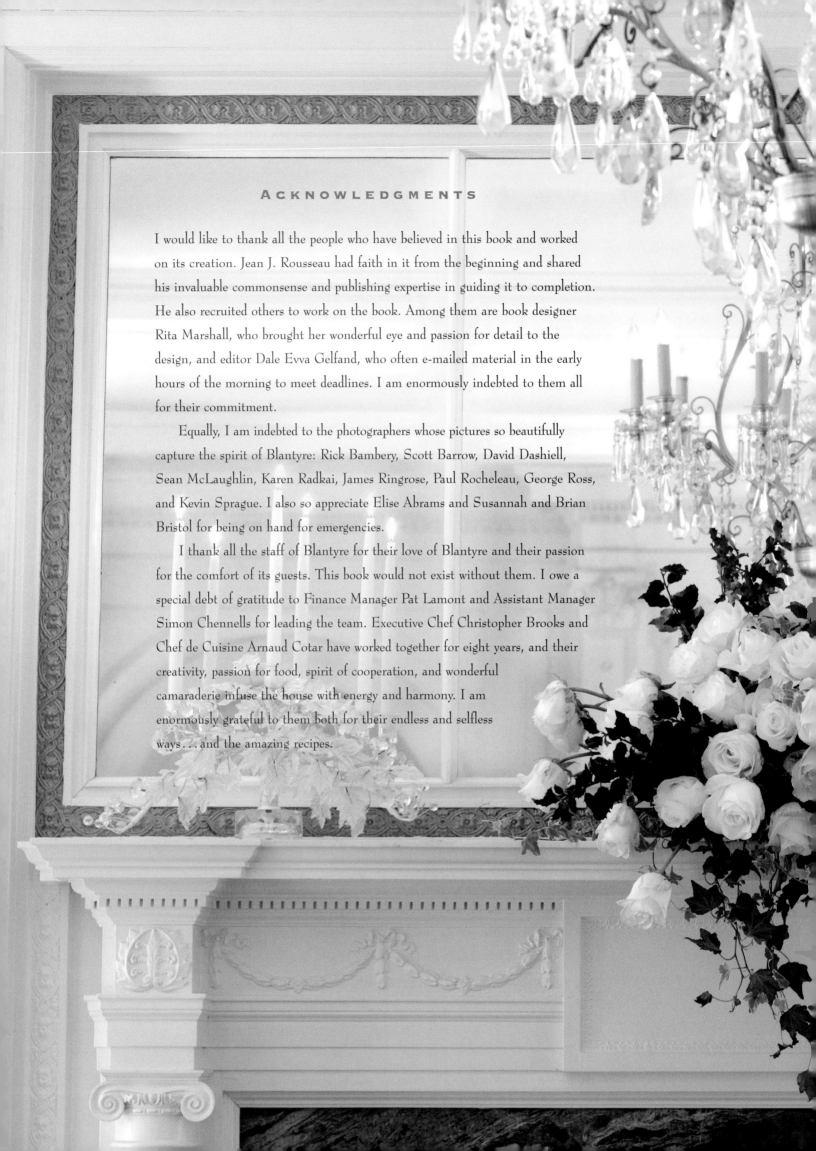

ACKNOWLEDGMENTS

I would like to thank all the people who have believed in this book and worked on its creation. Jean J. Rousseau had faith in it from the beginning and shared his invaluable commonsense and publishing expertise in guiding it to completion. He also recruited others to work on the book. Among them are book designer Rita Marshall, who brought her wonderful eye and passion for detail to the design, and editor Dale Evva Gelfand, who often e-mailed material in the early hours of the morning to meet deadlines. I am enormously indebted to them all for their commitment.

Equally, I am indebted to the photographers whose pictures so beautifully capture the spirit of Blantyre: Rick Bambery, Scott Barrow, David Dashiell, Sean McLaughlin, Karen Radkai, James Ringrose, Paul Rocheleau, George Ross, and Kevin Sprague. I also so appreciate Elise Abrams and Susannah and Brian Bristol for being on hand for emergencies.

I thank all the staff of Blantyre for their love of Blantyre and their passion for the comfort of its guests. This book would not exist without them. I owe a special debt of gratitude to Finance Manager Pat Lamont and Assistant Manager Simon Chennells for leading the team. Executive Chef Christopher Brooks and Chef de Cuisine Arnaud Cotar have worked together for eight years, and their creativity, passion for food, spirit of cooperation, and wonderful camaraderie infuse the house with energy and harmony. I am enormously grateful to them both for their endless and selfless ways . . . and the amazing recipes.

Blantyre has had five General Managers who have all loved the house: Christophe Bergen, Michaela Lang, Roderick Anderson, Katja Henke, and Dennis Barquinero. Their work and passion helped make Blantyre what it is today. I am grateful to them all.

I also want to say a special thanks to Debbie Sweeney, who has been my Country Curtains assistant through thick and thin for over twenty years. Much gratitude also goes to the people of Country Curtains who have worked with my parents since 1954. They have supported and laughed and worked with me since I was five years old.

Lastly to writer Claire Hopley, whose passion for research and kind ways created and guided this book so beautifully: Thank you, Claire

Ann Fitzpatrick Brown

Jean Rousseau suggested to Ann Fitzpatrick Brown that I might write this book. I want to thank him for his confidence in me, and Ann for agreeing to trust me. I know it was a leap of faith for her, and I can't say how glad I am that she made it. Working with her has been a pleasure, and writing the book has been both interesting and fun. I have learned a lot too; not least from Executive Chef Christopher Brooks, who shared his recipes and was always generous with his time and advice. Thanks to him, and to all the staff at Blantyre for their helpfulness, kindness, and courtesy, and to Rita Marshall for being a pleasure to work with. And, as always, thanks to my husband Bob for everything he does to help.

Claire Hopley

INTRODUCTION

Quotations since 1981 from Blantyre's Treasured Guest Books

The Guest Books' pages testify to the joyful feelings that embrace this enchanting country house hotel and the warm spirit created by a gracious and friendly staff. Here to introduce Blantyre and this book are some of the guests' thoughtful tributes.

"Wonderful experience, terrific staff, helpful, pleasant, friendly, always there to assist, thank you." ❦ "Blantyre's reputation brought us here, but it is the staff that will bring us back." ❦ "Gosford Park without the murder." ❦ "Blantyre is a work of art." ❦ "We feel totally at home."

"I'm sorry I'm not leaving, I'm waiting to be taken on as staff and I'll be here forever."
"After a weekend at Blanyre celebrating our 40th Anniversary, my wife and I feel as if we are dating again." "You certainly know how to spoil people who are already spoiled." "New Year's Eve dinner was the most superb and the party was a cross between English grandeur and Venetian fun." "Our dogs loved it and we did too! Please send us a bill for the hole in the couch!" "Thank you for preserving a way of life that is vanishing." "We have been coming for years and have loved every moment, but this year was the best, my son paid." "Blantyre's elegance is not expressed in any sort of opulence. On the contrary, the emphasis falls firmly on an enveloping warmth and the kindness of the staff." "We shall return."

To Jack and Jane Fitzpatrick
with heartfelt thanks, glowing admiration
and love from their daughter Ann

CHAPTER ONE

THE BERKSHIRE COTTAGES OF THE GILDED AGE

Millionaire businessman Robert Warden Paterson — a well-known collector of oriental and ancient art — was sixty-five and his wife, Marie Louise — the music-loving daughter of a millionaire manufacturer — was forty-five when they moved into their newly built home, Blantyre, in 1903. They had both traveled — Paterson widely — and at that point they had an annual round: A few months were spent in Europe, collecting art and visiting such friends as Andrew Carnegie (during the 1890s they had a shooting box near Carnegie's Skibo Castle in Scotland). Then in June they were salmon fishing at the Patersons' lodge on the Cascapedia River in Quebec. Fall found them in New York at their home on West 51st Street (later at East 58th Street). After Christmas, they escaped the northern winter in the southern warmth of the Jekyll Island Club in Georgia.

The club was described in the February 1904 issue of *Munsey's Magazine* as "the richest, the most exclusive, the most inaccessible club in the world." It had only one hundred members, all of them wealthy, including J. P. Morgan and Joseph Pulitzer as well as Rockefellers, Goodyears, and Vanderbilts. Like the Patersons, most Jekyll Island Club members owned Manhattan mansions, and some, including Morris K. Jesup of Belvoir Terrace and John Sloane of Wyndhurst, owned summer homes in the Berkshires. So in 1900, when the Patersons decided to build a house in Lenox, Massachusetts, they were stepping into a life already shaped by Berkshire County's residents, many of whom were friends and acquaintances.

Andrew Carnegie

J. P. Morgan

Morris K. Jesup

George Westinghouse

Nathaniel Hawthorne

Just as Wordsworth and other Romantic poets had retreated to England's Lake District for inspiration, American writers and artists were among the first to find a haven in the Berkshires.

Herman Melville

Berkshire Beginnings

Why did so many wealthy entrepreneurs who accumulated vast fortunes during the Gilded Age build large and lovely houses in the Berkshires?

Their houses ranged from the lavishly affluent to the sumptuously grand. Nonetheless, their owners called the houses "cottages" and themselves "cottagers" to evoke the country life and pastoral pleasures. The Berkshire countryside was perfect for enjoying these delights in domestic splendor. Beautiful yet still relatively undeveloped, it was within easy access of New York, Boston, and other cities.

Bounded in the east by the Connecticut River and in the west by the Hudson River, the Berkshires were the last part of Massachusetts to be settled by colonists. Stockbridge was founded in 1734 as a mission to the Mohicans. Lenox was incorporated in 1767. The earliest settlers were farmers and merchants, but by the early nineteenth century, Lenox had sawmills, textile factories, glassworks, quarries, and an ironworks plus the affluent city visitors who were beginning to discover the charms of the Berkshires. The lovely scenery ranked high, and the clean, bright air and cool summers delighted those who lived in towns and cities dark with coal smoke and rank with smells from factories and garbage. Indeed, since medicine then had few weapons in its arsenal, many visitors came to the Berkshires for the health benefits of pure air. The extension of the Housatonic Railway in 1838 brought Lenox within easy reach of New York and Boston; nevertheless, Lenox and Stockbridge (which the railroad reached in 1850) remained definitely rural rather than suburban.

Writers and Artists

Just as Wordsworth and other Romantic poets had retreated to England's Lake District for inspiration, American writers and artists were among the first to find a haven in the Berkshires. Nathaniel Hawthorne, whose best-selling novel *The Scarlet Letter* lifted him from obscurity to fame, arrived in 1850, when he withdrew to Lenox to write in peace. During his eighteen months in the area, he met Herman Melville, then living at Arrowhead Farm in Pittsfield and writing *Moby Dick*, which he dedicated to Hawthorne. Hawthorne, meanwhile, was writing *Tanglewood Tales*, a retelling of Greek myths for children. The word "Tanglewood" evokes Berkshire County's woodlands, and William Aspinwall Tappan liked it so much that he adopted it for the small house Hawthorne had rented from him; then, in 1866, he called his newly built residence Tanglewood, too. (In 1937 his heirs donated it to the Boston Symphony Orchestra, whose summer home it still remains.)

Numerous other artists also spent time in the Berkshires, among them actress Fanny Kemble, sculptor Daniel Chester French, painter Thomas Cole, and Hawthorne's college classmate Henry Wadsworth Longfellow. Writing about the artistic joys of his Stockbridge home, Longfellow exclaimed: "What a lovely place! . . . I build many castles in the air and in fancy many on earth."

Novelist Edith Wharton, who was building The Mount in 1902 while the Patersons were working on Blantyre, also voiced the artistic benefits of Lenox. During her first eager years of ownership, she wrote: "Lenox has its usual tonic effect on me & I feel like a new edition, revised and corrected . . . in the very best type." She sold The Mount in 1911 when her marriage was breaking up, but in her 1934 autobiography, *A Backward Glance*, she credited her days there with shaping her career:

> The Mount was to give me country cares and
> joys, long happy drives through wooded lanes of
> that loveliest region, the companionship of a few
> dear friends, and the freedom from trivial obliga-
> tions which was necessary if I was to go on with
> my writing. The Mount was my first real home . . .

Henry Longfellow

Numerous other artists also spent time in the Berkshires, among them actress Fanny Kemble, sculptor Daniel Chester French, painter Thomas Cole, and Hawthorne's college classmate Henry Wadsworth Longfellow.

Edith Wharton

The Mount

After visiting Lenox, novelist Edith Wharton wrote, "I am in love with the place, climate, scenery, life & all." In 1902 she and her husband, Teddie, built The Mount, a cottage she had helped design. She called it her "first real home." It gave her the freedom to write and to enjoy "the companionship of a few dear friends," most famously her mentor, Henry James, who visited The Mount several times. Though she sold The Mount in 1911, she noted in 1934 that "its blessed influence is with me still." In 2002 the Mount and Blantyre celebrated their centennials together with a dinner at Blantyre.

its blessed influence is with me still.

The freedom from trivial obligation, so important to Edith Wharton, appealed to many others. Some, like Wharton, had grown up in cities, cosseted by wealth yet restricted by the exacting social round it imposed, and a Berkshire house was a sanctuary, where freely chosen pleasures replaced stringent duties. Others, like George Westinghouse of Erskine Park, Morris K. Jesup of Belvoir Terrace, and Robert Warden Paterson of Blantyre, had made their own fortunes, and for them a Berkshire cottage was one of the rewards of hard work.

Berkshire Cottages and Cottagers

Samuel Grey Ward is credited with building the first of the Berkshire cottages. A member of a Boston banking family, he had published poetry and essays and belonged to the Transcendental movement founded by Ralph Waldo Emerson, whose adherents also included Nathaniel Hawthorne. Following Emerson's dictum "Build, therefore, your own world" as a way to spiritual growth, the Wards longed to escape humdrum urban stresses. Visits to Samuel's friend Willie Sedgwick, who lived in Stockbridge with his novelist sister, Catharine Sedgwick, fostered the Wards' love of the Berkshires. In 1844 they bought a site overlooking Lake Makheenac and built Highwood. Modest by later "cottage" standards, Highwood was designed by Richard Upjohn, a prestigious New York architect, and was a substantial Italianate house — not a cottage in any ordinary sense.

Like Highwood, most of the early cottages were relatively unassuming. They were designed for families that wanted many bedrooms for guests, ample terraces for outdoor summer living, and extensive grounds for games and riding. However, these early and relatively modest cottages soon gave way to increasingly elaborate and imposing residences.

Cottagers spared no expense on land and gardens, buildings and interior decoration. Bellefontaine, for example, imitated the Petit Trianon, the mansion Louis XV built for Madame de Pompadour.

By the end of the nineteenth century, Berkshire County — especially the towns of Lenox and Stockbridge — had some seventy-five cottages, including the immense Shadow Brook, completed for Anson Phelps Stokes in 1894, and the palatial Bellefontaine, completed for Giraud and Jean Van Nest Foster in 1898. In 1900, when the Patersons decided to build Blantyre, such splendid residences had pushed the price of buildable land in Lenox to $20,000 an acre, compared to only a few dollars per acre in nearby farming communities.

The cottages sometimes changed hands. After building Highwood, Samuel Grey Ward then built Oakwood in 1876. Anson Phelps Stokes

In 1900, when the Patersons decided to build Blantyre, such splendid residences had pushed the price of buildable land in Lenox to $20,000 an acre, compared to only a few dollars per acre in nearby farming communities. In this early picture of Blantyre, the wing on the right is the art gallery, which is shown from another angle on p.31.

Cornelius Vanderbilt

Starting with a single Staten Island ferryboat, Cornelius Vanderbilt built one of the first Gilded Age fortunes by investing in shipping and railroads and speculating in the stockmarket. His eldest son, William H. Vanderbilt, doubled the family wealth. William's daughter Emily Vanderbilt Sloane inherited $10 million. In 1886 she and her husband built the palatial Elm Court, from where Emily reigned as social leader of the Berkshires' summer colony.

bought the Oakwood estate, used the acreage to build Shadow Brook — then the largest house in America — and converted Oakwood itself into stables. When Spencer P. Shotter visited the Patersons at Blantyre, he decided that he, too, wanted a Lenox home — and he acquired Shadow Brook in 1906. He later sold it to Andrew Carnegie, who died there in 1919.

A few cottagers regarded their Berkshire property as their primary home; most did not. Either way, they all had several homes: townhouses in New York or other cities, oceanside mansions in Newport or Bar Harbor, sometimes even property in Europe. The Patersons, with their New York house, Scottish shooting box, and fishing lodge on the Cascapedia River in Canada, were not at all exceptional. Nor were they unusual in taking frequent trips to Europe. They might well have met their Massachusetts neighbors on a transatlantic liner or in a London or Paris hotel.

The Gilded Age

Where did all the money come from to support this lifestyle, which demanded dozens of servants, perfect clothes, elaborate well-stocked stables, jewelry, and eventually new-fangled automobiles.

Edith Wharton was relatively unusual in that her family's fortune went back several generations. Many cottagers inherited money from entrepreneurial immigrant fathers or grandfathers. Charles Astor Bristed of Lakeside was descended from John Jacob Astor, a German immigrant who arrived in 1784. He made money first as a fur trader, then by trading furs for silks and tea in the Far East. Finally he became a real-estate king, having bought much of Manhattan when it was farmland. He lived to see it covered with houses, whose rents amounted to $270,000 a year. The Vanderbilts — including Emily Vanderbilt Sloane, who owned Elm Court in Lenox, and Frederick Vanderbilt Field of High Lawn — were descended from Cornelius Vanderbilt, who parlayed a Staten Island ferry-boat into a steamship business that prospered enormously from carrying prospectors to the California gold mines. Already a multimillionaire, Vanderbilt moved into railroads after the 1862 Homestead Act opened up the West and while the Civil War demand for moving troops and materiel was at its height.

The Civil War was indeed a fertile field for anyone wanting to harvest a fortune. The demand for weapons, uniforms, tents, blankets, leather, wagons, ships, locomotives, and foodstuffs was unprecedented. Numerous entrepreneurs rushed to supply the demand — Robert Warden Paterson among them. Often they had little capital, but hard work, cleverness in making the most of opportunities, and fearlessness in the stock market made them enormously wealthy. Andrew Carnegie of Shadow Brook is the most iconic. Like Paterson, he left Scotland as a child. During the Civil War, he ran railroads and the Union telegraph service. In 1870 he opened his first blast furnace in Pittsburgh, and by the 1880s the Carnegie Steel Company was the world's largest steel manufacturer. Paterson, today more obscure than his friend Carnegie, owned one of the two largest naval stores exporting firms in the world, and was also involved in chemicals, insurance, and banking.

Wealth from such ventures enabled Berkshire cottagers to lead lifestyles that were opulent by any standard — glaringly so, given the poverty of many Americans. Observing this phenomenon, some writers praised the American energy that had created the wealth, often using Darwin's theory of evolution to justify the survival of the economic fittest. Silas Lapham, the entrepreneur hero of William Dean Howells's *The Rise of Silas Lapham*, says, "There's no doubt but money is to the fore now. It is the romance, the poetry of our age." On the other hand, in the classic economic text of 1900, *The Theory of the Leisure Class*, economist Thorstein Veblen accurately characterized the spending behavior of the wealthy as "conspicuous consumption." Historians now refer to

Robert Warden Paterson

The Patersons, with their New York house, Scottish shooting box, and fishing lodge on the Cascapedia River in Canada, were not at all exceptional. Nor were they unusual in taking frequent trips to Europe. They might well have met their Massachusetts neighbors on a transatlantic liner or in a London or Paris hotel.

the period from roughly the 1870s to 1915 as the Gilded Age — an epithet adapted from a book by Mark Twain and Charles Dudley. The word "gilded" rather than "golden" suggests the gleam and glamour of money — but also its tendency to disappear: Gilding wears off.

Indeed, the era of the Gilded-Age cottages of the Berkshires was relatively brief, spanning seventy-five years. Blantyre was among the last cottages to be built. Robert Warden Paterson died in 1917, just fourteen years after moving into Blantyre, and by the time Marie Louise Paterson sold it in1925, numerous other cottagers were also disposing of their huge properties, unable to finance their formerly lavish lifestyle.

Many of these grand private houses have disappeared — some burned, some demolished.

Others have found new uses as museums, schools, and resorts. Blantyre survives as a lovely and lively model of that Gilded Age life that elsewhere proved so transient. As Steven M. L. Aronson noted in the July 2004 *Architectural Digest*, "Itself no longer a private house, Blantyre is perhaps an even better thing — a country-house hotel dispensing the kind of service, cuisine, and décor that only luxury tempered by good taste can bring into being."

Despite the acumen that built a thriving business, a great fortune, a prestigious art collection, and a lovely home to display it in, Robert Warden Paterson is little remembered today. He did not establish charities that might have kept his name alive — unlike neighbors such as Andrew Carnegie and Morris K. Jesup of Belvoir Terrace, a founder of the American Museum of Natural History and an important financial supporter of both the YMCA and Arctic explorations. Nor did Paterson donate his art collection to a museum, which would have preserved it intact. After the death of his wife Marie Louise in 1938 the paintings, ceramics, and objets d'art were auctioned by Parke-Bernet and dispersed.

CHAPTER TWO

THE HOUSE THAT TURPENTINE BUILT

Pioneering Years

While names such as Rockefeller, Morgan, Westinghouse, Carnegie, Astor, and Vanderbilt still stir memories of the Gilded Age, few have heard of Robert Warden Paterson. Who were the Patersons who built Blantyre and what were they like?

Robert Warden Paterson was born in Dundee, Scotland, in 1838, the eldest surviving son of James Paterson and Ann Warden Paterson. When Robert was four, the family emigrated to Canada, settling near Toronto. His father worked in textile mills until 1852, when an illness forced him to change careers and farm the acreage he had bought — apparently sight unseen — in Euphrasia, Ontario.

The Patersons thus became pioneers in a region Canadians still called "the bush." There were no roads and few settlements. "Everywhere the great forest reigned supreme," wrote the local newspaper, the *Meaford Monitor*. Nonetheless, the family set about building a log home. Gradually other farmers — most of them Scottish like the Patersons — moved in, and the rocks and forest were cleared.

Financially, the Patersons thrived, not simply by farming but by running a store, whose success the newspaper attributed to "Mrs. Paterson's exceptional aptitude for mercantile pursuits." Ann Paterson also had twelve children, eight of whom survived to adulthood. Knowing that his mother had helped establish the family in Canada, it's not surprising that Robert Paterson often sympathized with the problems women faced. In his 1900 book, *Impressions of Many Lands*, he alludes to the lives of women in every country he visited, often praising the greater freedoms of American women.

The Patersons and their orchestrelle

Out on His Own

In his early twenties, Robert Paterson left his family's forest home and traveled to Oil Springs, near Petrolia, Ontario, where in 1858 a well digger had struck an oil gusher. Entrepreneurs flocked there, setting off the world's first oil boom and transforming Oil Springs from a hamlet of two or three houses into a village of 3,500 people. Once again Robert Paterson became a pioneer.

Perhaps encouraged by Americans he met in Petrolia, or simply noting that the Civil War was creating even bigger opportunities over the border, in 1863 he emigrated for a second time, heading down to New York and setting up as a lumber merchant in Brooklyn. By 1869 a Brooklyn business directory listed him as a naval stores merchant. "Naval stores" refers specifically to tree products such as rosin and turpentine derived from longleaf and other pines. Wooden sailing ships used them for treating ropes and waterproofing. Naval stores were also in demand for new Industrial Age products such as soaps, detergents, varnishes, paint, and linoleum. America was the world's biggest supplier of naval stores, most of the production coming from trees grown in Georgia and Florida.

Paterson's business grew quickly and included importing as well as exporting. Besides his New York City headquarters, he opened offices in such ports as Mobile, Savannah, and Wilmington as well as in Europe. Some idea of the company's reach comes from employee Edmund Nash (the father of poet Ogden Nash). Writing to his parents in 1882, Nash described his business itinerary: "Antwerp, and thence to Amsterdam & Rotterdam, Mainz, Berlin and Cologne. Then Hamburg, Stettin, Danzig, Warsaw, Riga, St. Petersburg & Moscow. Leaving there I will go to Southern Europe, then to Paris, England again, Scotland and *home*. That is quite a trip isn't it?"

Eventually Paterson's company grew so large that on November 18, 1906, the *Atlanta Constitution* called it one of "the two greatest naval stores exporting firms in the world." The other was the S. P. Shotter Company. The two companies merged in 1906 to form the American Naval Stores Company, based in Savannah. At this time the federal government was accusing naval stores companies of restraining trade under the Sherman antitrust legislation. The case received huge publicity, not least because, as the *Atlanta Constitution* explained on February 6, 1907, the men involved were "the most prominent in naval stores in the world . . . men of great wealth and social prominence."

Family Life

While Robert Warden Paterson was building his company, he was also starting a family. In January 1866, he married Noble Dickson in Toronto. Like himself she had emigrated from Scotland as a child. Presumably Noble died because the 1870 census shows him living with his second wife, Emma Downing, and their month-old son, Henry.

Emma's parents, William and Mary, were from Brimfield, Massachusetts, but by 1870 the widowed Mary Downing was living at her sister's Brooklyn home near to Paterson's, so Emma and Robert probably met as neighbors. Certainly, the relationship between the two families was close. Mary Downing lived with Robert and Emma at times, while Emma's brother Albert became Robert's partner in Paterson, Downing and Company. Albert died when he was only 30. Emma also died quite young. The obituary column of the *Brooklyn Daily Eagle* of November 21, 1889 noted her demise: "Suddenly, at her residence, 286 Clinton Ave., Brooklyn, Emma Downing, wife of Robert W. Paterson, in the 45th year of her age." Thus, at 51 Robert Paterson was again a widower. He had two sons, Henry, now 19, and 8-year-old Robert Downing Paterson, who fell to his grandmother's care.

Travels

Paterson had become an American citizen in 1888. In his 1891 passport application he had to describe his appearance in lieu of the photograph required in today's passports. He was 5 foot 11, with a high forehead, gray eyes, black hair, and a florid complexion. He characterized his nose, mouth, and chin simply as "normal." Photographs show him bearded and mustached, with a forthright gaze and trim figure. He looks vigorous and energetic, which he needed to be for the two trips he took and wrote about in his book, *Impressions of Many Lands*. In 1892 he went to the Holy Land to visit biblical sites, followed by trips to Constantinople and Athens. In 1893 he went on a Far Eastern journey to India, Ceylon, Hong Kong, Japan, and Hawaii. He writes lucidly and with considerable ability to evoke scenery. His book shows him to be observant, knowledgeable, direct, and often opinionated. His account of the Holy Land reveals wide knowledge of the Bible and serious religious feelings. Perhaps most effectively and movingly, he connects biblical people with those of his own era. After fishing in the Sea of Galilee, for example, he ruefully notes the failure to catch anything and the speed with which a storm blew up, writing: "We realized something of what the disciples met with."

Whereas the visit to the Holy Land was often arduous, involving long mule-back desert journeys, the 1893 Far Eastern journeys was luxurious. He traveled in comfort, stayed in fine hotels, and dined with dignitaries. His comments about their lifestyle and the life of the countries he visited reveal his active mind. Considering Indian clothing, he writes: "We have seriously deteriorated in the matter of dress. To see these erect figures, both men and women, gliding gracefully past, in contrast with our own stiff movements, forces this thought on us. Here is nothing to impede the full use of every limb, and room is given for the full development of every part of the body as nature intended it should be." Ever the businessman, he reflects on Indian fields that had been farmed for thousands of years yet showed no signs of exhaustion, saying, "Well may . . . the world fear this formidable competitor, with such a soil, and wages 10 to 12 rupees or $3.00 to $3.75 a month and no food furnished."

Most interestingly, his collector's eye was engaged by the art of every country, especially the architecture. Fine workmanship and beautiful proportions always awed him. In Ahmenabad he notes, "These mosques and tombs are of red sandstone, and although small, are both architecturally beautiful, and exquisite in every detail of workmanship. There is a warmth of coloring about the red sandstone that gives it an advantage over the marble for certain kinds of chiseled work." When he later built Blantyre, it wasn't of sandstone, but its brick and brownstone have the warm color he admired, and the refined proportions of its rooms reflect his architectural sensibilities.

His respect for craftsmanship appears again in his discussion of Japanese lacquer. Here, his professional knowledge of tapping trees makes him especially appreciative: "Taking this black resinous substance, the gum from a species of sumac, they put coat after coat on a soft wood or paper surface, polishing each coat with infinite patience, and on the surface thus polished, form figures of bird, beast, man or landscape, using most skillfully, silver, gold, and ivory in their work; and the finished product is a masterpiece that is priceless." He reinforces this description with a tale of a shipwrecked cargo of lacquer that had lain on the seabed for eighteen months without suffering water damage. Usually, he encourages haggling with dealers, but writing of lacquer, he says, "Any curio hunter who can unearth any of these treasures does well to possess himself of them without regard to price." His own art collection included a brown lacquer smoker's cabinet and a spectacular lacquer chest inlaid with ivory and decorated with flowers, birds, and legendary figures.

One aim of the Far Eastern journey was to buy such objets d'art. He chose well. When his art collection was sold in 1938, the Parke-Bernet catalog noted that the prized white jades of eighteenth-century China were "represented . . . superbly in the Paterson collection." It also singled out many of his Chinese ceramics as masterpieces, extolling the "remarkable technical skill" of some pieces and describing his blue-and-white hawthorn vases as "magnificent."

Marriage and Honeymoon

Impressions of Many Lands is organized as a series of letters. Presumably he sent them to Marie Louise Fahys, whom he married in December 1893, shortly after his return from the Far East. His book dedication describes her as: "The companion of my life and of my wanderings whose sympathetic appreciation of my letters gave birth to this volume."

Like Emma Downing, Marie Louise Fahys was a neighbor, the thirty-six year-old daughter of Joseph Fahys, who had emigrated from Belfort, France, in 1848 when he was sixteen. After apprenticing to a watch-case maker, he prospered and married *Mayflower*-descendent Maria Payne of Sag Harbor in 1856. Their eldest child, Marie Louise, was born in Hoboken in 1857. By 1866 Fahys owned two watch-case factories, and in1902 he was employing a thousand people in his Sag Harbor factory, which eventually became the Bulova watch company. The family lived in Gilded Age luxury. They summered in Sag Harbor, often cruising on their yacht *Alsace*. In winter they lived near the Patersons on Clinton Avenue. Joseph Fahys was a trustee of the Lafayette Avenue Presbyterian Church, which Paterson had attended since arriving in Brooklyn in the 1860s. Indeed, he and Fahys were probably friends since Fahys was his senior by only six years.

Marie Louise and Robert Paterson had what the *Brooklyn Daily Eagle* of December 5, 1893, termed "a quiet wedding," with only fifty people sitting down to the wedding breakfast. Despite the barrenness of a northern December, thousands of flowers decked the house. According to the *Eagle*:

> A particular feature of the wedding was the elegance and beauty of
> the floral decorations. The large reception room in which the cere-
> mony took place was banked with palms relieved by thousands of
> pink roses, while the windows and mantels were filled and covered
> with maidenhair ferns and chrysanthemums. The parlors where
> the breakfast was served were decorated entirely in white, bridal
> roses, ferns, and palms predominating. From the chandeliers and
> floral candelabra on the tables, chains of smilax interwoven with
> white roses and hyacinths were artistically draped.

Photographs of Marie Louise at the time show her as soft featured, with light hair pulled back from her face. For her wedding she wore a gown of white satin trimmed with old lace, and she carried white roses and lily of the valley. Roses remained a favorite flower, often mentioned in later newspaper descriptions of Blantyre. (Today, lush arrangements of roses in every shade of pink and white still adorn the house.) As for the chrysanthemums that decorated the Fahys' mantels, the Patersons' Blantyre gardener would become a nationally renowned grower of them.

The Patersons spent their honeymoon wintering abroad. *Brooklyn Daily Eagle* Paris correspondent Emma Bullet caught up with them in their hotel drawing room on May 6, 1895. Passing quickly over such treasures as Egyptian coffee cups carved out of carnelian and paintings by Jules Dupré, Bullet focused on their acquisitions in Paris, "home of all that is desirable." She praised Paterson's taste in having the gems he had bought on his journeys set Parisian style so the gold — "the ugly yellow metal" — was invisible in the "many rings" and a bracelet of sapphires of varying colors he gave his new wife. Marie Louise also displayed her new and extensive wardrobe from Jacques Doucet, renowned as the first French couturier to use delicate, filmy fabrics such as supple silks and laces.

Marie Louise Paterson

A Gilded Lifestyle

Shortly after the marriage, the Patersons moved from Brooklyn to a more prestigious home on West 51st Street in Manhattan. By now Robert Paterson, who was involved in a number of businesses — mostly lumber related — with his brothers, had become treasurer of a new phosphate-mining company in Florida. He was also a principal in the New York chemical company Paterson, Boardman and Knapp, and eventually became a director of the Manhattan Bank.

Paterson displayed equal fervor for nonbusiness pursuits. An angling enthusiast, in 1897 he jumped at the chance to buy a half share in William Mershon's camp and fishing rights on the Cascapedia River in Quebec. Soon he built his own camp, called The Bungalow. As co-owners of shared rights on the river, Paterson and Mershon often fought rivals for ownership of prime salmon-fishing territories. But though they were allies, Paterson was the opposite of the outgoing Midwesterner Mershon, who complained to a fishing pal, "I wish Paterson was a little more companionable, and our kind of people. He is a good fellow, but rather cold-blooded, and there is not much fun in him." Whether this was the taciturnity of the stereotypical Scotsman or the reserve of the high-powered businessman, his cold-bloodedness suggests some reserve in Paterson that manifested in his focus on his business, his art collection, and the building of Blantyre.

The Patersons of Blantyre

The appeal of Lenox, Massachusetts, to Robert and Marie Louise Paterson was immediate. A September 3, 1904, article called "Charming Blantyre" printed in *Berkshire Resort Topics* — a Pittsfield newspaper devoted solely to the doings of summer residents — reported: "Mr. and Mrs. Paterson first came to the Lenox in October 1900, and were so delighted with the resort that their determination to make it their permanent summer abode was soon announced."

Lenox was neither as formal or grand as Rhode Island's Newport (though it was sometimes called "the inland Newport"), nor as artistic as neighboring Stockbridge, nor yet, according to Andrew Carnegie's wife, Louise, as hectic as Bar Harbor, Maine — another

popular summer destination. She explained that Lenox had a social life for those who wanted it, but, she added approvingly, "one can be independent." People amused themselves with games, walks, rides, and convivial gatherings. Some returned for Christmas house parties, occasionally staying into winter for tobogganing, sleigh rides, and hockey, even visits to forest sugaring shacks, where Thomas Cole painted some of them gazing into cauldrons of boiling maple sap.

Robert Paterson bought 130 acres planted with specimen trees and including a house and service buildings from George Dorr (known as "the Father of Acadia National Park"). The parcel, spread delightfully across a

In this view of Blantyre, the art gallery wing can be seen behind the trees at the left. For unknown reasons, the gallery was removed some time in the 1930s. For another view of it, see page 17.

Originally, the walls of the Main Hall were covered with embossed bronze wallpaper. This now appears only in the stairwell and on the landing outside the Paterson Suite, where the undamaged sections of the original paper have been pieced together. Other changes to the Main Hall include the magnificent oriental carpet. In most ways, however, the room remains much as it was in the Patersons' day.

hillside with views of Laurel Lake was purchased in Marie Louise's name, as was more acreage bought later. But while she legally owned the property, Robert largely directed the building of Blantyre, hiring New York architect Robert H. Robertson to design it in the style of an Elizabethan manor.

Then as now, the entrance to the house was along the graceful turns of the driveway leading to the porte cochere and thence into a vestibule that opens onto the Main Hall. It had two plant rooms at the corners opposite the door. "Running among the plants are myriads of miniature electric lights, which in the evening illuminate the rooms in a most entrancing fashion," enthused the writer. (Today one Plant Room, still shaded by palms and gardenias, serves as the business nook, while the

Louise and Andrew Carnegie

second Plant Room harbors Blantyre's pre-dinner drinks, including a collection of single-malt Scotches and Armagnacs, some of them over a half century old.) The Conservatory housed palms, ferns, and flowers, making it "one of the most attractive features of the house," in the eyes of the *Berkshire Resort Topics* reporter.

Like the house, the furniture was English. The Main Hall had copies of pieces in the Tudor palace Hatfield House. The Reception Room had Adam-style furniture custom made in England, while London-based Gillow and Company provided Jacobean-style dining-room furniture. The large "music room and library," decorated in green and white and furnished with Sheraton-style furniture, had "many fine paintings." Other items from the Patersons' art collection included a Gobelin tapestry in the dining room, Flemish tapestries in the doorways, a massive oak table in the Main Hall, and English suits of armor and antique weapons displayed about the house.

During the two years it took to build Blantyre, the Patersons planned exactly where the furniture was to go so that on delivery it was immediately set in its preordained place. In 1917 Andrew Carnegie and his wife, Louise, were living at nearby Shadow Brook because his failing health prevented them from traveling to his beloved Scottish home. Louise was thrilled to spot similarities to Scotland, writing to a friend: "The Patersons' house and furnishings are so Scotch, I feel I have crossed the ocean and am in Scotland itself on a fine estate."

The Paterson Art Collection

This similarity to British county houses was no accident. By the time the Carnegies visited, the Patersons had hung the house with paintings chosen to emphasize its Britishness. The most important group was a collection of eighteenth-century English and Scottish portraits by Gainsborough,

Andrew Carnegie and his wife, Louise, bought Shadow Brook in 1917 because Andrew's failing health prevented them from traveling to Skibo Castle, his beloved home in Scotland. Louise Carnegie was anxious that he should not pine too much for Scotland, so when they visited his old friend Robert Warden Paterson at Blantyre, she was thrilled to find it so congenial. "The Patersons' house and furnishings are so Scotch, I feel I have crossed the ocean and am in Scotland itself on a fine estate," she wrote.

The Patersons not only chose English furniture for their house, they also bought British landscapes and eighteenth-century portraits such as George Romney's The Stanhope Children, *shown opposite. Though dressed in white frocks with blue sashes, the children are boys. The elder (on the right) is Charles Stanhope, Viscount Petersham. Born in 1780, he inherited the title Earl of Harrington. Both he and his younger brother, Lincoln, on the left, became major generals in the British Army. In the 1938 auction of the Patersons' art collection, this painting fetched $5,000, making it one of the most valuable that they owned. This painting can be seen displayed to the left of the window in the photograph of the Patersons' gallery on page 36.*

Reynolds, Romney, Raeburn, and Morland. But by far the greatest number of paintings were idyllic landscapes, among them eight Constable watercolors, Highland scenes from Scotland, and paintings by Corot and members of the French Barbizon school. Many of these include cows and sheep, reinforcing Blantyre's rural setting. One or two paintings, such as Isabey's *The Defense of the Castle*, show armed knights — complementing Paterson's suits of English armor — while the occasional seascape like Felix Ziem's *The Golden Horn, Constantinople* would have reminded Paterson of his visit there.

Notably, virtually all the paintings disposed of in the sale of the collection after Marie Louise Paterson's death in 1938 were bought in 1903 or later for display in Blantyre's art gallery. Paterson was already a well-known art collector, but he had focused on the decorative arts: Chinese pieces in porcelain, jade, teak, and ivory; Japanese lacquer; French fans and miniatures; English furniture and silver; Belgian tapestries; oriental carpets; and Hispano-Moresque majolica. His decision to buy paintings was clearly motivated by the wish to decorate Blantyre elegantly.

Unfortunately, none of Paterson's paintings remain at Blantyre today; but, coincidentally, current owner Ann Fitzpatrick Brown bought impressions of engravings that Paterson had also owned: five scenes of married life by J. R. Smith after George Morland. Similarly, Blantyre's current collection of paintings — "not so famous but wonderful," Ann calls them — includes eighteenth and nineteenth-century portraits and landscapes, several of them featuring the cows that were such a Paterson favorite. The similarity of her tastes and the Patersons' suggests both the magic of Blantyre and Ann's empathy with the house that has kept alive its century-old spirit.

George Romney's The Stanhope Children

Art Gallery with Romney's The Stanhope Children *displayed on the back wall on page 36*

Larger Art Gallery

The Patersons bought several eighteenth-century portraits by English and Scottish artists, among them Thomas Gains-borough's Mrs. Burroughs *and* Sir John Campbell *(seen above and displayed in the art gallery on page 38). Gains-borough was the favorite portrait painter of George III, yet he began as a landscape painter and often longed to return to that genre. His landscapes, which Constable much admired, were represented in the Patersons' collection by* A Gypsy Scene. *In the 1938 sale of the art collection, it sold for $1,400, while* Mrs. Burroughs *fetched $2,100 and* Sir John Campbell *went for $2,900 — tiny figures by today's standards.*

Blantyre's Grounds and Gardens

Robert Paterson planned the grounds of his home with the same thoroughness he devoted to the structure itself. His Scottish gardener, Thomas Proctor, laid out twenty-five acres of rolling lawn and created a formal English garden 250 feet long by 50 feet wide on the lowest of the three terraces in front of the house. His domain included a range of nine connected greenhouses — the most advanced of any in Lenox. The writer of "Charming Blantyre" explained: "They are built on absolutely new lines, being entirely of cement and glass with no wood being utilized except for the doors. They cover a space 175 feet square, are heated in the most approved style by hot water pipes, and are lighted by electricity."

Greenhouses were an established feature of the Berkshire cottages, providing out-of-season delicacies such as peaches and grapes as well as masses of flowers for drawing rooms and dinner tables. Many cottagers, including the Patersons, invested heavily to grow exhibition blooms. But even with serious competition from other cottagers, the reporter clearly saw the Patersons' greenhouses as exceptional. Conversely, the stable block, though big enough to accommodate sixteen horses, had "no particular effort centered on it." Already the motorcar was taking over. Robert Paterson was an early member of the American Automobile Association

The Naming of Blantyre

Having planned a house in a region of cottages with charming names like Tanglewood, Pine Needles, and Merrywood, the Patersons must have debated what to name it. Paterson's ultimate choice was based on memories of his early years in Ontario. The town of Euphrasia where James Paterson had settled his family gradually developed a new township with its own post office and James Paterson as post master. The township and its post office was called Blantyre at the suggestion of a neighbor who had been born in Blantyre, 8 miles south of Glasgow in Scotland. By naming his beautiful Massachusetts home after the Ontario village where his father had prospered, Robert Warden Paterson both affirmed his links with the old country and his family's success in the New World.

Life at Blantyre

So, with a lovely house, evocatively named and surrounded by gorgeous gardens, how did the Patersons spend their time? Like most Berkshire cottagers, they were peripatetic. In the winter they spent two months in their Manhattan home, described in "Charming Blantyre" as "a veritable museum with antiques and curios from Egypt, Palestine, Turkey, Greece, China, and Japan." They still traveled to Europe after building Blantyre, but they also took advantage of Robert's election to the prestigious Jekyll Island Club close to Savannah, Georgia, which was the base for Paterson's export business.

The season for fishing the Cascapedia was June. Marie Louise Paterson also fished. The *New York Times* reported that during the 1907 season, she caught one salmon weighing thirty-five pounds and another of thirty-six pounds. These huge fish were packed in boxes of ice and shipped home to Blantyre, where they would have been stored in the ice house (now Blantyre's Ice House Cottage).

The Patersons arrived in Lenox a little later than some cottagers but in time for the seasonal festivities. Chief of these for Robert was golf, and Lenox had four or five tournaments a year. In 1903 he won an August tournament and was still playing in late October, when *Berkshire Resort Topics* described him as "among those most frequently seen on the links." His photograph appears at the top of the page alongside that of Teddie Wharton, Edith Wharton's husband.

Though the Berkshire Hunt Club rode over the Patersons' land — which totaled 230 acres after additional purchases in 1903 and 1904 — apparently the Patersons didn't participate in Lenox's equestrian events. The most popular was the September Tub Parade, a procession of pony carriages festooned with flower garlands. July 4 saw a similar event on Lake Mahkeenac, with flower-decked boats celebrating the holiday. Robert Warden Paterson was on the Board of Governors of the Lake Mahkeenac Boating Club (where Ann Fitzpatrick Brown is now a member).

The flowers in their greenhouses regularly took prizes at the Lenox Horticultural Society's shows and beyond. Noting that the principal flowers to be shown at a 1904 show were "chrysanthemums, roses, and orchids from the large greenhouses together with violets, carnations, and many other products," the local newspaper cited Paterson as "among the chief exhibitors."

He had an expert gardener in Thomas Proctor. In 1908 the *Boston Globe* described Proctor as "the foremost grower of chrysanthemums in New England, and one of the most expert culturists in the country." He had won the Chrysanthemum Society of America's cup in New York in 1907 for the best vase of twenty-five flowers. In 1908 he won another national cup in Chicago, and at the Lenox Horticultural Society show he scooped up more prizes for his chrysanthemums and first prizes in every class he entered.

A few years later the *Boston Globe* was one of many newspapers that reported on Blantyre's clarkia, a flower native to the Rockies. On June 21, 1914, a reporter was thrilled with banks of the pink blooms "relieved with patches of small, purple, daisy-like chrysanthemums and orchids." The *New York Times* of June 14 noted that "Mr. and Mrs. Robert W. Paterson have been showing their friends some wonderful blooms of clarkia." A few days later the *Times* described a reception for Lenox public schoolteachers: Marie Louise played the orchestrelle (a water-powered pipe organ), Robert explained the paintings and ceramics, and "tea was served in the conservatory where Mr. and Mrs. Paterson are displaying a collection of pink clarkia, said to be the finest collection grown in this country, the double flower being developed at Blantyre." Proctor was the genius behind this. He also worked on new varieties of orchids, which can be seen in early photographs of the Conservatory, where they still thrive today.

Battling for honors in flower shows is typical of the competitiveness that infused much of the Berkshire cottagers' social life. They also loved displaying flowers on their tables, and newspaper reports of their entertainments often mention them. *The Berkshire Gleaner* of September 1903, for example, describes Blantyre's table adorned with Marie Louise's "favorite decorations of pink and white roses."

In contrast, newspapers rarely mentioned what people ate — a tantalizing omission, given today's interest in food and cooking. Fortunately, hotel menus of the era give an

Clarkia Flowers

idea of the dishes in fashion during the Patersons' Blantyre days. Meals were built on ingredients and recipes that were long established in New England: lamb, beef, ham and chicken were equally popular. Though remote from the sea, Berkshire cooks could easily get fish shipped from the coast by the frequent train services. Investigators have unearthed huge piles of clamshells from the grounds of the old cottages, suggesting the popularity of clam chowder and steamers. Oysters were favorites, too, usually served scalloped or stewed rather than raw. They were also cheap; lobster was more luxurious for high occasions. Salmon was also a luxury in those days before salmon farming made it common. Shad, another fish that swims up rivers in late spring, was a seasonal treat. Fine poultry such as duck and guinea hen were much appreciated. Asparagus and green peas were summer luxuries; tomatoes and beets were also favorites. Strawberries, blueberries, and peaches were as beloved then as now, and pies reigned on dessert menus: apple pie, of course, but also rhubarb pie in spring, squash and pumpkin pie in autumn, and mincemeat pie throughout the year, not just at Thanksgiving. Wine jellies were another popular dessert.

Menus also offered items now rarely seen. An 1875 menu from Stockbridge House included cowslip greens. In 1908 the Red Lion Inn offered the newly invented health foods cornflakes and shredded wheat as appetizers. And in those days before the native chestnut trees were destroyed by disease, hot boiled chestnuts from Monument Mountain were a fall specialty.

These dishes were designed to appeal to cottagers' guests, who were often accommodated in hotels when guest bedrooms overflowed. The recipes appeared in standard cookbooks such as *Miss Leslie's Directions for Cookery*, published in Philadelphia in 1837, and its later rival, *Fannie Farmer's Boston Cooking School Cook Book*, published in Boston in 1896. Not that Gilded Age tastes remained unchanged. In the mid-nineteenth century, the cottagers preferred unsophisticated meals to reflect

On June 21, 1914, the Boston Globe described the flowers of Blantyre. Banks of clarkia "relieved with patches of small, purple, daisy-like chrysanthemums and orchids" thrilled the reporter. Paterson was clearly tremendously proud of the clarkia, which is mentioned in several articles published that year.

the simple rural life. By the Patersons' time, homey dishes were being replaced by French dishes — or if not actually replaced at least appearing with French names. A menu for a Pittsfield dinner in 1898 describes its lamb chops as *Côtelettes d'Agneau*, its oysters in white sauce as *Hûitres Bechamel*, and its chicken salad as *Salade de Volaille*.

Berkshire groceries stocked fine foods for the cottagers. But for special events, such as weddings, calls to Sherry's and Delmonico's in New York summoned their arrival with marquees and all the delicacies the city offered. At the Patersons' housewarming reception in September 1903, Sherry's orchestra played among the palms of the south terrace. After being greeted by the Patersons in the Music Room, guests could wander the house and grounds to the Conservatory to drink tea or chocolate.

Conservatory in the Patersons' day

Marie Louise Paterson was "at home" every Friday afternoon, when she would serve tea to visitors. Like other cottagers, the Patersons had frequent luncheon and dinner parties. They also hosted musical evenings. Then as now, the Music Room had a grand piano, and the organ was built so that a large audience could hear it, as explained in a *Boston Globe* article of June 21, 1914:

> The first art gallery is a step or two lower than the front portion
> of the house. On one side of this gallery is a beautiful pipe organ —
> an instrument [that] Mrs. Paterson plays — and in the other and
> larger gallery, high on the farther wall, is the echo instrument of

Conservatory today

Music Room in the Patersons' day

The upholstered sofa in the center of this view of the Patersons' Music Room is the only piece of their furniture still at Blantyre. It lay derelict when the Fitzpatricks bought the house. Ann Fitzpatrick Brown had it refurbished, and it is now in the Ribbon Room, as shown in the photograph above.

Marie Louise Paterson was "at home" every Friday afternoon, when she would serve tea to visitors. Like other cottagers, the Patersons had frequent luncheon and dinner parties. They also hosted musical evenings. Then as now, the Music Room had a grand piano, and the organ was built so that a large audience could hear it.

this organ. So that when both galleries are crowded, and when
some eminent organist is giving a concert here, all may hear the
music clearly and distinctly.

One of the few photos of the Patersons at Blantyre shows Marie Louise seated at the instrument with her husband standing proudly by. It is reproduced on page 23.

End of an Era

With the ability to entertain handsomely, a place to display their art collection, green-houses to nurture flowers and delicacies, golf courses for playing a favorite sport, and a chance to live in a society that had created an amusing series of annual events, Blantyre gave the Patersons a lovely setting for their last years together. She became a noted host-ess. He took care of their art collection — a task he reserved for himself. Though he had created numerous businesses and made lots of money, his life — like most — was not without shadows. Federal prosecution of the turpentine trust led to business problems. Two wives died young. His older son's divorce seems to have led to estrangement, while his younger son, Robert, was largely brought up by relatives in Montreal. Nonetheless, Paterson led a life of achievements. He founded and built up several businesses and helped his brothers get started in business. He became a respected art expert, with detailed knowledge of many of the arts of the Far East and antiquity. At a time when even the wealthy did not travel beyond Europe, he made a point of traveling in the East and writ-ing a book about his experiences. One of the few surviving copies is inscribed to his friend Andrew Carnegie, evidence of his admiration for a compatriot and an immigrant entrepreneur — a man very much after is own heart.

Robert Warden Paterson died at age 79 in his New York home. Following a service at the Lafayette Avenue Presbyterian Church, where he had long worshipped, he was buried at Sag Harbor on Long Island.

Dining Room in Patersons' day

CHAPTER THREE

BLANTYRE: FROM FORTUNE TO MISFORTUNE

Blantyre as a Tax Burden

It had cost the Patersons $135,000 to build Blantyre, not counting furnishings and fittings. In comparison, Edith Wharton's nearby home, The Mount, and Samuel Frothingham's Overlee, which were built at the same time as Blantyre, cost $40,000 and $100,000 respectively. Yet in 1925, little more than twenty years after its completion, Marie Louise Paterson sold Blantyre for only $25,000 — "the most sensational drop in real estate values in the history of Lenox," according to the local press.

Why did she do it?

The *Berkshire Eagle,* reporting the sale on April 1, described the property as "unoccupied" since Robert Paterson's death in 1917. Perhaps lacking her husband's enthusiasm for golf, Marie Louise found little to amuse her in Lenox. She had always traveled, often to France, and such trips could have rivaled Blantyre for her time and money.

Undoubtedly she was finding it increasingly expensive to maintain the house. In 1904 *Berkshire Resort Topics* reported that the Patersons had paid $1,888.70 in property taxes to the town of Lenox — higher than taxes on many other cottages though less than the taxes on Bellefontaine, Ventfort Hall, and Blantyre's neighbor, Wyndhurst (now Cranwell Resort). But in a June 14, 1916, article headlined "Lenox Biggest Taxpayers are Women," the *New York Times* reported that "Mrs. Marie Paterson, wife of Robert W. Paterson of Blantyre, is assessed on the most valuation of any Lenox property this year. The Board of Assessors have levied $321,000 on personal and real estate held by Mrs. Paterson, and the tax is $5,150." (By comparison, palatial Bellefontaine paid the next highest tax: $4,485; Wyndhurst paid $4,368.)

The art collection explains the steep tax bill. The Patersons had bought paintings continuously, beginning in 1903. Blantyre's art gallery also housed many of the ceramics and artifacts that Paterson had acquired earlier. The difference between the taxes of 1904 and 1916 reveals the value of the art displayed at Blantyre and suggests why Marie Louise Paterson lent most of the paintings to the Brooklyn Museum in 1920. Certainly she was anxious about taxes. Having turned down $250,000 for Blantyre in 1920, believing it to be worth more, she sold it for a tenth of that just five years later, reputedly explaining that she had "to let it go before the taxes ate it up."

Marie Louise was not alone in her problems. By 1925 the river of revenues from the Gilded Age economy flowed less ebulliently. The Civil War, Reconstruction, and the opening up of the West by railroads had drummed up vast fortunes, but by the early 1920s that drumbeat sounded only faintly. The new income tax of 1913 had depleted the millions that had built the Berkshire cottages. Antitrust laws had reined in numerous businesses, including those of both Marie Louise's father and her husband. Quite simply, few people sailed on the flood tide of Gilded Age fortunes any longer.

Blantyre as The Wyndhurst Club

Howard Cole, of New York and Palm Beach, Florida, purchased Blantyre. He also bought Wyndhurst, Coldbrook, Pinecroft, and Belvoir Terrace — all at fractions of the prices they would have fetched a few years before. Their aggregate land amounted to more than a thousand acres. Cole planned to use the properties as a country club called The Wyndhurst Club. Blantyre was to be the clubhouse.

He began well enough, quickly completing work on a nine-hole golf course and inaugurating the club with a grand dinner. Looking back on it in 1939, a reporter for the *Berkshire Eagle* wrote, "Members of the summer colony of the southern Berkshires . . . were present. It was a great day for Lenox, and many of the town's residents looked forward with

In a 1914 Boston Globe *article describing a visit to Blantyre's art gallery, the reporter said that "Mr. Paterson prizes very highly" this terra cotta Madonna and Child by Andrea della Robbia. The figures are exquisitely modeled in white relief against a blue ground, surrounded by a green-and-yellow border of fruit and flowers. The writer noted "It is undoubtedly the best example of this sixteenth-century sculptor's work in the United States. It was found in Spain and in order to secure it, it was necessary to purchase the old church in the wall of which it was embedded."*

eager anticipation to the day when The Wyndhurst Club would be the center of activity for the socialites of the East."

It never happened. Cole walked into a quicksand of financial problems. A string of lawsuits from mortgage companies and unpaid contractors led to foreclosure and the sale of the club in 1928.

Blantyre as The Berkshire Hunt and Country Club

Woodson R. Oglesby, a former congressman from Yonkers, New York, acquired Cole's properties for $220,000 — about half the tax assessor's valuation. Blantyre alone was assessed at $146,000.

Oglesby shared Cole's vision of a grand country club, but liking the cachet of the word "Berkshire" and the prestige of fox hunting, he changed the name to The Berkshire Hunt and Country Club. He advertised plans for a pack of fox hounds, a polo field, an airstrip, and an elaborate swimming pool, and he actually laid out miles of bridle paths, a show ring, and hurdles for jumping.

Unfortuntely, like Cole, Oglesby failed to create the club he had envisioned. He might have succeeded twenty or thirty years earlier. Lenox's summer residents had always loved sports, especially British games like golf, tennis, croquet, cricket, and equestrian activities, including fox hunting. In 1896 Anson Phelps Stokes and other summer residents had founded The Berkshire Hunt Club, modeled on English hunts such as the Quorn, with whom Stokes hunted during the winter. But hunting is expensive. As the stock market crash of 1929 spiraled into the Great Depression of the 1930s, Oglesby descended into debt.

Foreclosure threatened until film director D. W. Griffith came to the rescue by paying the taxes. In return he became club president, writing to members that he was "heartily in sympathy with the plan to establish on a firm basis The Berkshire Hunt and Country Club as a recreational and sports headquarters of major proportions."

Edward Cranwell held a second mortgage on the club's properties. As financial problems again mired Oglesby and Griffith, Cranwell waited for the bank to foreclose, then bought up the club. He didn't get Blantyre, even though the Wyndhurst golf course surrounded it, because Oglesby had deeded it to his wife. So Cranwell rebuilt the course, and Wyndhurst became the clubhouse. The club survived until 1939, when Cranwell donated it to the Jesuit order, which used it as a boys' preparatory school. The school closed in 1975, and the house became Cranwell Resort.

Blantyre as a Film Studio

Oglesby, meanwhile, was still unable to pay his property taxes on Blantyre. In 1938 the town of Lenox took possession, until D. W. Griffith, who had had a long association with Oglesby and was possibly a distant relative, once more played knight in shining armor by buying Blantyre for $1,000 — again agreeing to pay the outstanding taxes and penalties.

Griffith now planned to use Blantyre as an eastern outpost for the film industry. Reportedly he was looking for a suitable New England story to film. But after a year he sold it back to Oglesby, who lived in it for a couple of years before selling it to Henry de Sola Mendes.

Blantyre as an Inn

Henry de Sola Mendes owned a summer camp in Becket. At first he used Blantyre to accommodate his campers' visiting parents, but in 1946 he expanded it from a seasonal guesthouse to a full-scale inn that served both out-of-towners and the local community. (Local residents could become members for $50 a season or pay $2.50 for a day's use of the facilities.) He installed a huge swimming pool (above the present croquet lawn), and hosted dinner dances that appealed to both guests and local residents. The combination of a local clientele, guests who enjoyed the inn, and his strong sense of Blantyre as a digni-fied house enabled de Sola Mendes to succeed for more than twenty years, where others had failed.

Blantyre as The Tanglewood Tennis and Pool Club

Henry de Sola Mendes retired in 1968 and sold Blantyre to Robert P. Weiss and Lee

Gunst of New York, who immediately began a modernization program. They installed three tennis courts and renamed the property The Tanglewood Tennis and Pool Club. Inside, they turned what had been the Patersons' music room into a restaurant called the Oak Room, decorated with wine-colored fabrics and carpets. A year later they converted the carriage house into a fourteen-unit guesthouse, and the following year they remodeled the conservatory, using white wicker and yellow-topped wrought-iron tables to recreate the atmosphere of a late-Victorian garden room. The next step was the development of the Below Stairs bar and discotheque, outfitted with of the latest stereo and audio equipment plus witty murals adapted from Mary Petty's *Tweeny the Maid* cartoons in *The New Yorker*.

But despite the popularity of the discotheque among Berkshire County's young people, all the improvements left no money for taxes, and in 1976 the Lenox Savings Bank foreclosed on the property, becoming its owner as the sole bidder at the public auction sale.

Blantyre as a College Campus

In 1977 the bank sold Blantyre for $332,000 to John Donohue, president of Mark Hopkins College in southern Vermont. He claimed to be creating a second college campus at Blantyre and applied for funding grants. But within a year he was awash in troubles. Not only was the Lenox Conservation Commission insisting that the ailing drainage system be repaired, in February 1979 Mark Hopkins College sued Donohue, "seeking damages and the recovery of federal funds allegedly stolen." With a tangle of lawsuits, tax liens, mortgages, and penalties enmeshing his property, Donohue could neither sell Blantyre nor raise funds to maintain it.

Yet again, the Lenox Savings Bank foreclosed. Blantyre's owners seemed fated to run into financial troubles.

D.W. Griffith

Born in Kentucky in 1875, David Llewellyn Wark Griffith yearned to be a playwright. In 1907 he went to California, hoping to sell a script to the burgeoning film industry. He failed, but he was hired as a director in 1908. By 1915 he had made 450 short films, many of them in a little village he discovered called Hollywood. He then made The Birth of a Nation, *the first American full-length feature film. It was enormously profitable, though its depiction of racism was controversial. In response, he made* Intolerance, *which attacked slavery. In 1919 he collaborated with Charlie Chaplin, Mary Pickford, and Douglas Fairbanks in founding United Artists. His only sound films were* Abraham Lincoln *(1930) and* The Struggle *(1931). Griffith, shown opposite at Blantyre, hoped to make the house into the film-making center of the East. He died in 1948.*

CHAPTER FOUR

THE HOUSE THAT CURTAINS RESTORED

A New Splendid Age

Looking back from 1979, when Blantyre was in foreclosure for the third time, to 1916, when it had been the most valuable house in Lenox, it is hard not to think that it had been dogged by the misjudgments of many of its owners. Some were misled by the will-o'-the-wisp of grandiose club plans; others were foiled by costly modernizations. However, when Jack and Jane Fitzpatrick bought Blantyre in 1980, they ushered in a splendid era that has already lasted much longer than those fourteen gilded years when Robert and Marie Louise Paterson spent summers at their Lenox home.

The Fitzpatricks and Paterson share crucial common qualities. Like Paterson, the Fitzpatricks are entrepeneurs. They founded Country Curtains in 1956 as a home-based mail-order company selling traditional ruffled muslin curtains. Jane Fitzpatrick drew a little picture of the curtains and sent it as a small advertisement to *American Home*. At a cost of only $2.50 a pair, they flew off the shelves, and Country Curtains thrived from the beginning. In 1958 the Fitzpatricks moved Country Curtains to Stockbridge, Massachusetts — still its home base — where it has grown to be one of the most successful mail-order businesses ever.

The Fitzpatricks share Paterson's love of collecting paintings, ceramics, and other art objects. Jane Fitzpatrick regularly attended auctions, bidding so frequently and successfully that one local auctioneer said, "It's better to behold Jane Fitzpatrick with her paddle up than have a rainy day." She made a point of acquiring many pieces from the great Berkshire houses that were being closed or demolished during the '70s, and '80s, accumulating a huge collection of items, some of them now gracing Blantyre's rooms.

Jack and Jane Fitzpatrick

In 1957 Jane and Jack Fitzpatrick brought their infant Country Curtains business to Stockbridge. They have always given back to the community where they prospered and which they love. They have spread their generosity widely, with a special focus on Tanglewood and the Boston Symphony Orchestra and the Berkshire Theatre Festival. In Stockbridge they were close friends with Norman and Molly Rockwell, and later became founding members of the Norman Rockwell Museum.

Meanwhile, Jack Fitzpatrick — who served as a State Senator from 1972 to 1980 — loved buying real estate as much as Jane loved buying pictures and antiques. In 1968 he and Jane bought the Red Lion Inn in Stockbridge, and Country Curtains became a tenant, using part of the ground floor as retail space. The Fitzpatricks later bought nearby houses to use as hotel annexes and, in 1976, a failing textile mill in Housatonic, which they refurbished as the Housatonic Curtain Company making curtains for Country Curtains. When they bought Blantyre, Jack Fitzpatrick told his younger daughter, Ann, "We're buying this hotel. Have fun with your mother fixing it up."

Blantyre as a Country House

By this time the Fitzpatrick family had been running the hundred-room Red Lion Inn for twelve years. Though they had come to the task as neophytes — "On the day we bought it, I realized I now had seventy-five bathrooms to clean," laughs Jane Fitzpatrick — they soon turned the 1773 Stockbridge landmark from a failing enterprise into one of the most popular inns of New England.

Blantyre gave the Fitzpatricks a new stage for their skills and talents. Fortunately, Robert Paterson had built Blantyre to high standards, and it had remained reasonably sound. It had escaped fires that devastated the interiors of Bellefontaine and burned Shadow Brook and Ashintully to the ground. The roof did not have holes as did Ventfort Hall, and the house hadn't suffered prolonged spells of emptiness. Even so, Blantyre needed an enormous amount of work.

The earlier efforts to convert it into an inn and restaurant had inspired decor summed up by Jane Fitzpatrick as "red-plastic chairs." Much of this had to be undone. More substantially, when financial crises trapped Blantyre's previous owners, they simply stopped maintaining the house. Some idea of its condition comes from the *Berkshire Eagle* of

Moire Room

May 30, 1981, which reported general contractor John Oppelaar's description of the interior when the Fitzpatricks started work: "A horror show of cobwebs, sunken ceilings, torn screens and shutters, broken windows, vandalized wood carvings, rotten floors, burned mantelpieces, water-stained walls, warped wooden panels, chipped plaster reliefs, and neglected artwork."

Fortunately, their thriving Country Curtains business gave the Fitzpatricks the where-withal to tackle these and Blantyre's other problems. Seventy-five percent of the plumbing system had to be replaced and the whole house rewired. The roof needed major repairs. It took a ton and a half of copper to fix drainpipes, gutters, and cracks through which water leaked and damaged rooms below, including the plaster ceilings. The hall ceiling lay under the bathroom in the Paterson Suite, where the floor had rotted down through sixteen inches of concrete and joists. The floor had to be torn out, yet the ceiling had to be preserved — a task achieved by laminating in new joists. Chipped moldings throughout the house required repair, and tiles in damaged fireplaces needed replacement.

Inventiveness succeeded where replacement was impossible. For example, to repair the laurel bands of the Moire Room moldings, the contractor made casts of those that survived, sprayed silicone into the casts, then filled them with automotive plastic to create new leaves that could be attached to the original moldings. To replace the plaster relief on the ceiling, he used a similar stratagem, using window-glazing putty for molds. Broken tiles on the fireplace in the Corner Suite could not be reproduced, so the sound ones were refitted into complete rows, and the mantel was lowered. The original wallpaper on the second-floor landing was retained by removing the few remaining undamaged sections from the staircase and fitting them in. Beyond such skilled tasks lay a multitude of simpler but time-consuming jobs. Doors and sconces had eight coats of old paint stripped off, the oak paneling on the staircase was refinished, lights had to be scraped to uncover the brass, and plain old elbow grease was needed to polish the brass hardware on doors and windows. Four servants' rooms were converted into two bedrooms, each with a bathroom. Where original fittings remained in the bathrooms, they were restored. When necessary, items in a complementary style were added to preserve the look of the house as it had been in the Patersons' day. Sometimes the originals were given new life. One of the Patersons' sofas lay derelict in the basement. Refurbished to the standards that its first

Fairlawn Room

Crimson Suite

Laurel Suite

Corner Room

Fernbrook Room

Windyside Suite

Maplehurst Bathroom

Fernbrook Bathroom

Blue Room Bathroom

Blue Room Bathroom detail

owners would have demanded, it now sits in the Ribbon Room.

All this repair and conservation work prepared the way for sumptuous furnishing and decoration. Jane and Ann Fitzpatrick were pre-armed with a treasury of antiques that they had been buying over the years. They continued buying, choosing furniture, carpets, pictures, china, silver, glass, lamps, and ornaments because they liked them and they suited the house.

Ann shares her mother's decorating principles. "My mother has always said that you must have beautiful lamps and mirrors — and we do," she says. The Tiffany lamp in the Music Room is a brilliant example. It was presented to Blantyre soon after opening by Ann's father, a lover of Tiffany lamps.

Like the lamps, the chandeliers delight the eye. The Dresden chandelier over the table in the Breakfast Room is a flowery fantasy. The crystal chandeliers of the Music Room are scintillating showers. The golden chandeliers that once shone in Ann's New York apartment now enrich the airy spaces of Blantyre's Conservatory, reflecting the plants and flowers in their garlands and in the roses and irises that cradle the lightbulbs.

Discussing the lavish draperies that hang on Blantyre's windows, Ann Fitzpatrick Brown says, "My mother and I both felt that the draperies should look like ball gowns." Thus, damask, silk, velvet, and moire descend in fulsome folds, flounced with swags, trimmed with fringes, looped back with tasseled cords.

"The idea is to make Blantyre as comfortable as possible, as if one were staying in one's own home," Jane Fitzpatrick told the *Berkshire Eagle* reporter when Blantyre reopened. A glance at the visitors' book on the Main Hall table proves how well she and Ann have succeeded. Again and again, guests write their appreciation of the comfort of the rooms, the delights of awaiting dinner in the Music Room or by the fire in the Main Hall, their sense of being nurtured by the splendor and kind spirit of the house.

Looking back on the year of intense work to bring Blantyre back to life as a Gilded Age mansion, Jane Fitzpatrick mused, "To preserve an old estate in the Berkshires is a very satisfying endeavor. It makes you feel good."

Dresden Chandelier in the Breakfast Room

Tea in the Music Room

Tea in the entry of the Carriage House

Blantyre Relives

Blantyre opened its doors to guests on June 1, 1981, just a year after the Fitzpatricks began work on it. From the outset visitors fell in love with the scrupulous and sumptuous renovation. But work has never stopped.

Ann Fitzpatrick Brown moved straight from dealing with refurbishment and decoration to planning and creating new facilities. The swimming pool installed by Henry de Sola Mendes in the 1950s had cracked, and Jack Fitzpatrick insisted it spoiled the view, anyway. So in 1982 Ann had the pool removed and two championship croquet lawns installed. (She later built a new pool, nestled beside the Potting Shed Spa, which is connected to the Carriage House.) She also refurbished the four tennis courts, one of which is original to the house, as is the 1920s tennis court roller, which is still in regular use.

In the 1970s Robert Weiss and Lee Gunst had created fourteen rooms in the former carriage house. Renovation of these began in 1982 and has continued ever since. The aim has been to give each room its own unique personality and to make them as inviting as the rooms and suites in the Main House, with antique furnishings, objets d'art from the Fitzpatricks' collections, lovely wallpapers complementing luscious draperies, and libraries of DVDs and books.

Believing that books "warm a room," Ann Fitzpatrick Brown began collecting them for Blantyre in 1999, often taking a group of friends on book-buying trips to make sure that she gathered volumes that appeal to differing interests. She comments, "They are so important. One is never alone with a book." Now every room in Blantyre has a myriad of volumes, some of them handsome books on art, ceramics, houses, and gardens; others include biographies, poetry, and novels. Every room has at least one children's book.

The most recent addition to the Carriage House block is the Potting Shed Spa, designed by Stockbridge architect Pam Sandler and opened in 2005. While some guests love the experience of being in the Patersons' Gilded Age mansion and opt to stay in the Main House, others choose Carriage House rooms so they can escape easily to the pleasures of the spa. Here, surrounded by windows with views across sloping lawns to sheltering trees, they can relax in gentle waters. Floating there on a brilliant winter day when snow

Potting Shed Spa and Pool — a haven lovingly overseen by Lynne and her staff.

Greenhouse Hot Tub

Pool in summer

Treatment Room

swirls outside is like being inside a snow globe. It is just as lovely when the trees flutter with the pale leaflets of spring or shade the lawns in summer or flaunt their paint-box colors in fall. As for treatments, the spa fosters the sense of well-being that typifies Blantyre, with massages, wraps, facials, pedicures, and a waterfall shower to relax aching muscles.

En route from the Carriage House to the Main House are four cottages. Starting in 1982 with the Riverview Cottage and the Old Bath House Cottage, then moving on to the Cottage by the Path in 1984, and finally in 1999 the Ice House — where the Patersons stored their salmon in the old days — Ann Fitzpatrick Brown has made each one a unique and private place. Frank Macioge of Lenox was the architect for two of the cottages: the Riverview and the Ice House.

Many of the old china vases and bowls that the Fitzpatricks bought on their auction visits are now essential equipment for Blantyre's florists, who pack them with the flowers that are a Blantyre hallmark. Stargazer lilies adorn the dining-room sideboard; bowls of pink roses — sometimes studded with snapdragons, sometimes cushioned by peonies — sit on the tables. In late winter, tall white tulips or long branches of forsythia on the Music Room table promise spring. Later, the first lilacs perfume the air as guests listen to the evening's pianist. Orchids reign in the Conservatory just as they did in June 1914, when Robert Paterson told a *Boston Globe* reporter that these "aristocratic floral babies" need the right air because "they are very delicate and uncertain." As much as the Conservatory suits orchids, Ann says, "Bouquets of flowers suit Blantyre." Like Marie Louise Paterson, she loves pink and white roses. (She's not quite so keen on the chrysanthemums the Patersons' gardener bred so successfully.)

Indeed, Blantyre has become the splendid country house it is today because it is the work of a discriminating sensibility. That sensibility is Ann Fitzpatrick Brown's. In part it comes from her training as a sculptor. In her twenties she created a business called Gumdrop Square, which made joyful, candy-covered structures. The grandest work was a one-ton candy castle for Macy's flagship Manhattan store. The skills that made a creation like that possible also come into play when she decorates a room. Comparing rooms to candy sculptures, Ann says, "I think of both as a collage of textures, patterns, and colors." This suggests how the mixture of fabrics, furnishings, paintings, books, and antiques at Blantyre come together as a harmonious whole. The humor that prompted the candy sculptures plays a role, too. From the fancifully rampageous rocking horse in the hall to the jeweled rabbits that snuggle together as breakfast salt and pepper shakers, Blantyre elicits smiles to gild the satisfaction of being indulged by plump pillows, charming bibelots, the prettiest of flowers, and the most memorable of meals.

Winter Wonderland

Since 2005 Blantyre has been open year-round. This reflects Ann Fitzpatrick Brown's conviction that in many ways the house glows brightest in winter. Certainly when nights draw in, the wind blows, and snow flies, few consolations satisfy as deeply as the log

Ann and Alexander Brown

Ann Fitzpatrick Brown's son Alexander, seen here 7 months old, may be seen carrying bags, answering the phone, and greeting guests during school vacations.

When asked which job at Blantyre he was aiming for he replied, without hesitation and with a big smile, "My mother's!" His photograph appears on page 91.

fires in the Main Hall and Dining Room, the comforts of the rooms or suites, many with fireplaces of their own, and the certainty that there is no need to go outdoors.

On the other hand, lots of pleasures await there. Snowshoes and cross-country skis invite guests to explore the snowy landscape, and flooded skating rinks entice them to glide across the gleaming surface. They can follow this fun with fondue or cups of hot chocolate served with Executive Chef Christopher Brooks's homemade marshmallows and banana bread. Sometimes there's a Snow Barbecue, with oysters on snowballs and Scotch Toddy Marinated Steak to celebrate the season.

Turning Blantyre into a winter retreat was another of Ann's projects for constant improvement. Never built for winter, the house had to be winterized and skis and snowshoes provided for everyone, plus a Zamboni (pulled by a lawn tractor) was needed to keep the ice in perfect shape for skating. In 2006 the Warming Hut was built as a cozy haven for those who ventured forth into the snow. It has welcoming armchairs to rest in and a pool table for indoor sport — facilities that are just as welcome in summer.

Being open in winter means that Blantyre's guests literally see the Berkshires in a new light. Days can be brilliant, with blue skies arching over the sparkling white beneath, or they can be gray and filled with swirling snow as the warmth of the house draws itself around its residents.

Grand Events

The year Ann's son, Alexander, was born — 1989 — was also a great year for French wines. Ann remembers, "My first wine purchase was an Imperial of 1989 Château Pétrus for $17,000 for Alexander's twenty-first birthday. I was shocked with myself and was convinced I could never tell my parents! But my fascination with wine had begun. The wine

Warming Hut

world and Blantyre were now forever lovingly entwined."

One of the first tasks that Ann undertook when she became owner of Blantyre was a visit to two of England's country house hotels, Gravetye Manor and Chewton Glen, so she could experience their special world. They were both members of Relais & Châteaux, the prestigious French association of family owned and operated hotels and restaurants. Located in various countries, all are intimate and based in old mansions, castles, hunting lodges, manor houses, and camps. Blantyre proudly became one of the first three American members of Relais & Châteaux in 1983.

Since 2003 Blantyre has had a five-star Mobil rating. It had four from 1991 to 2002, and Ann Fitzpatrick Brown recalls the day when manager Katja Henke called to tell her that Blantyre had been awarded its fifth star. Ann recalls, "A group of guests arrived from Texas. They asked Katje to meet them outside. They had a camera. They announced that Blantyre was awarded its fifth star from *Mobil Travel Guide.* Shocked beyond belief, Katja asked, 'But why?' They said, 'Because everyone just loves Blantyre.'" Ann pauses. "I cried!"

Blantyre Today

Being overcome by emotion at hearing the news of that fifth star reflects Ann Fitzpatrick Brown's intense commitment to the house she loves. Her Blantyre isn't a strict recreation of the early-twentieth century taste of the Patersons, or a narrow collection of artifacts from one era, or a museum of decorative art — though those who love such places can spend happy hours appreciating the thousands of objects that make Blantyre such a visual delight. Rather, Blantyre is, as it was always intended to be, a country home filled with treasures chosen for their appeal and for their kinship with the house. Designed by the Patersons for comfort and relaxation during the last years of the Gilded Age, it basks now in a splendid age of infinite care for everything that makes life more delightful.

Ann Fitzpatrick Brown's son, Alexander, seen here with the Wheaten girls: clockwise from bottom left
Gracie, Ruby, and Mattie. The Wheaten girls have collaborated with Blantyre's chefs
on special menus and treats for their visiting friends.

CHAPTER FIVE

CHEF CHRISTOPHER BROOKS

Not least of the pleasures of Blantyre is knowing that a memorable dinner awaits at the end of the day, and morning will start with a leisurely breakfast, which guests can enjoy in their room or the flowery Conservatory. In either case it sets the stage for the pleasures of the day to come. The presiding genius of meals at Blantyre is Executive Chef Christopher Brooks. His cuisine is regularly singled out by restaurant and travel guides for their rarest and most glowing accolades. Zagat rated it the best in the Berkshires, and Blantyre invariably appears high on national lists of the best one hundred places to eat. Guests, too, write paeans in its praise in Blantyre's visitors' book. Quite simply, all agree that Christopher Brooks is a great chef.

His greatness springs from many sources: from talent, of course, but also from the cooking he grew up with at home in England, from his training in classic French technique, and from his work in the kitchens of several country house hotels and Relais & Châteaux properties in England and the United States. From these experiences he developed the culinary principle that guides his work: *Simplicity is the key to elegance.* This translates to the finest in-season ingredients treated reverently, often in the classical tradition but with modern verve and imagination. The aim is perfection — or, as Chef puts it, "as close to perfection as possible."

Chef Christopher Brooks

Dining Room

Executive Chef Christopher Brooks and Chef de Cuisine Arnaud Cotar seen here with the kitchen crew

Equally important as the food is his strong sense of the pacing and orchestration of a meal. Christopher considers the ambiance, the service, the wine — all the details. Dinner begins in the Music Room, where guests contemplate the menu as they sample canapés. Inventive and delicious, they are, in Chef's words, "the first experience of the meal; they leave the guest wanting more." The meal proceeds in the dining room, where flowers and elegant tableware set the scene for the dishes to come. The servers' smiles suggest that they know the secrets being prepared in the kitchen, and they can't wait to see the joy on the guest's faces when the set pieces of appetizer and main dishes arrive on the table. The grand finale is dessert: a virtuoso conjuration of flavor notes that always wins applause. Then comes a charming coda of chocolates and petits fours served with coffee — or perhaps a brandy or a cordial. Diners retire feeling not just entertained and replete, but cared for and cherished.

That sense of being nurtured, spiritually as well as physically, is rooted in home — and "home" is where Christopher returns when he explains why be decided on a career in cooking. "I used to cook Sunday breakfast with my dad, and my mum always used to cook everything from scratch," he says. "And I just love food." His parents supported his ambition, so the next step was training in a traditional four-year English apprenticeship at Chewton Glen, one of the oldest and most beloved of Britain's country-house hotels. Here Christopher spent five days a week getting hands-on experience of the workings of a first-class kitchen and learning skills from experienced cooks. He spent another day each week at college in Bournemouth studying food science and restaurant management.

After apprenticeship, he worked at Huntstrete House, the Relais & Châteaux property in Bath. "We used to grow most of the vegetables and some of the fruit," he recalls. He also worked at Foxhills in Surrey. Then in 1995 he came to America to continue his career as sous-chef at

The key to a successful kitchen is a strong core team who hand down their experience. Chef Brooks with Chef de Cuisine Arnaud Cotar (right) and Sous-chef Paul Pearson (left).

1945
Chateau Mouton Rothschild

Blantyre

1945
"Année de la Victoire"
Chateau Mouton Rothchild

December Wine Dinner
16th December 2007

Seared Scallop
with a Prawn Ravioli and a Carrot and
Shallot Nage

Cured Duck Breast
with Foie Gras, Huckleberries and a Pear Salad

Rack of Lamb
with Chestnut Croquettes, Buttered Cabbage,
Glazed Salsify and a Sage Jus

Lazy Lady Farm O' My Heart Cow's
Double Cream Cheese

Dessert Pastries in the Music Room

TENUTA DELL' ORNELLAIA

SPRING SUPPER

Blantyre

Ornellaia
Tenuta dell' Ornellaia
Bolgheri
Sunday, April 27th, 2008

Hors d'oeuvres
KRUG, "GRANDE CUVÉE", MAGNUM

Seared Monkfish
with Soft Polenta and Porcini Mushrooms
LE SERRE NUOVE, DELL' ORNELLAIA 2005 · 2004

Trio of Duck
Sous-Vide Breast   Confit   Foie Gras Cromenski
ORNELLAIA 1995 · 1997

Roast Spring Lamb
with Fontina Cheese and Leek Fondue, Carrots and
Crispy Potatoes
ORNELLAIA 2001 · 2003

Italian Cheese Tasting
Robiola Bosina   Toma
ORNELLAIA 2004 · 2005

Coffee and Pastries in the Music Room
ORNELLAIA, GRAPPA

KRUG

SUMMER TASTING SUPPER

Blantyre

KRUG
Summer Tasting Supper
June 22, 2008

Hors d'œuvres
KRUG "GRANDE CUVÉE"

Wild Salmon Pastrami
with Cucumber Panna Cotta and American Caviar
KRUG "CLOS DU MESNIL", BLANC DE BLANCS · 1996

Scottish Langoustine
with Morels, Fava Beans & Chervil Krug Foam
KRUG · 1996

Tenderloin of Veal baked in Salt Crust
with Orange and braised Veal Cheeks with
Preserved Lemon
KRUG ROSÉ

KRUG "CLOS D'AMBONNAY", BLANC DE NOIRS · 1995

Explorateur Cheese
with Cassis Jelly and Baguette
KRUG "GRANDE CUVÉE" MAGNUM

Coffee, Chocolates & Petit Fours in the Music Room
Chef Christopher Brooks ∞ Chef de Cuisine Arnaud Cotar

AUTUMN WINE SUPPER

featuring the wines of

BURGUNDY NEGOCIANT

CAMILLE GIROUD

Blantyre

Camille Giroud
November 5th, 2006

Hors d'œuvres
CHAMPAGNE, LOUIS ROEDERER
CHASSAGNE-MONTRACHET, LES VERGERS, 2004
VOSNE-ROMANEE, 2002

Celeriac Flan with Mâche Salad and Flat Bread
CRIOTS-BATARD MONTRACHET, EN MAGNUM, 2002

Pan seared Scallops with Parsnips Three Ways
CORTON-CHARLEMAGNE, 2004

Fall Lentils with Rosemary roasted Guinea Hen
and Guinea Hen Boudin
CHAMBERTIN, 2001 · CHAMBERTIN, 2002

Saddle of Lamb with Mushroom Brick & Winter Greens
VOSNE-ROMANEE, LES MALCONSORTS, 1978

Cheese Tasting with Autumn Fruits
LATRICIERES-CHAMBERTIN, 2002

Coffee and Chocolates & Petit Fours in the Music Room

∞

Chef Christopher Brooks   Sous Chef Arnaud Cotar

Blantyre. Later he worked in Dover Plains, New York, at the Old Drover's Inn and at the Morrison House Hotel in Alexandria, Virginia. In 2002 he was asked to return as Blantyre's Executive Chef.

Reflecting on his experience in so many kitchens, Christopher says, "They are all different. Over the years I've seen many characters in kitchens — some good, some not so good. You can find qualities in everyone you work with and learn from them — sometimes what *not* to do! You can always learn from people who have worked in other places, and you can use that knowledge. That's why this career is so good."

Among those he has learned from is his great friend Mark Payne, also a chef, who he says keeps him motivated. He also praises Arnaud Cotar, Blantyre's Chef de Cuisine. "Arnaud has a special place in my life," he says. "Since 2000 we have grown together personally and as chefs at Blantyre." Christopher points out that since Blantyre is open seven days a week, 352 days a year, he cannot be there all the time, so he needs Arnaud's strong support. "In my book, the Chef de Cuisine is a huge part of a kitchen's success," he says. "Arnaud and I share the same vision of food, and he always excels in what he achieves."

He also notes the achievements of Sous-Chef Paul Pearson, and in keeping with his sense that cooking is a cooperative art with everyone learning from everyone else, he says, "Every staff member makes the show continue; without them, it would not happen."

Looking further back to his own start at Chewton Glen, Christopher pays tribute to Pierre Chevillard, who guided his apprentice years: "He taught me all the basics. He gave me a wall that I could build on." Some of the building he does can be seen in Blantyre's changing menus. Explaining how they are created, Christopher says, "You need staples like lamb, beef, and so forth. Then we look at the foods in season and create a balanced menu. I always have pen and paper in my car in case I have an idea. And my kitchen crew always has input."

"Wine Director Christelle Cotar and Sommelier Luc Chevalier have quietly amassed one of the top cellars in the northeast. Every vinicultural base is covered and usually in depth."said Judith Grice and Randy Sheehan in a 2007 article on Blantyre in The Quarterly Review of Wines.

Since 2005 Blantyre's Wine Tasting Suppers have featured:

- *Chateau Montelena*
- *Fisher*
- *Arietta & Kongsgaard*
- *Camille Giroud*
- *Château de Beaucastel and Domaine Perrin*
- *Frescobaldi*
- *Château Haut-Bailly*
- *Château Mouton-Rothschild 1945*
- *Ornellaia*
- *Krug*
- *Château Haut-Brion*

Some menus appear on pages 98–99.

His crew also helps develop special menus, such as the Snow Barbecue, while the memorable dishes served at Blantyre's Wine Dinners come about after long consultations with the Wine Director Christelle Cotar and Sommelier Luc Chevalier.

Everybody has favorite dishes. Blantyre's kitchen has become famous for its foie gras preparations and toothsome scallops. For dessert, Christopher's Sticky Toffee Pudding, a favorite in England, is the runaway winner, and many guests are head over heels in love with his sublimely satiny Crème Brûlée (for recipes see pages 216 and 172 respectively). As for his own favorites, Christopher lists "a good English breakfast, tart tatin done well, whole roasted turbot, a big bowl of mussels with garlic and thyme and crusty bread, coffee ice cream."

Reflecting on the qualities needed to invent new dishes, develop intriguing menus, and run a top-flight kitchen, he lists "passion, creativity, common sense, discipline, and taste." And just as he owes his grounding to his own mentor, Pierre Chevillard, he says, "An Executive Chef has to be a father figure to his staff because a happy staff means happy guests and a creative kitchen."

With experience in many Relais & Châteaux kitchens, Christopher Brooks has an intense feeling for Blantyre. "Blantyre is special to me for many reasons. We are allowed to do things right. We have a great facility. We have enough staff. And we are always developing people, creating rising stars."

His final observation on the magic of Blantyre is that "Blantyre seems to bring people together." Undoubtedly the many guests who celebrate weddings, anniversaries and other special occasions at Blantyre would agree. For Christopher, this is especially true: In 1995 he met his Lenox-born wife when they were both working at Blantyre.

In November Christopher Brooks and his wife Amy attended the
2008 INTERNATIONAL CONGRESS OF RELAIS & CHÂTEAUX,
where it was announced that Chef Brooks had been elected to the
GRANDS CHEFS RELAIS & CHÂTEAUX.

Dining Room Sideboard

CHAPTER SIX

BLANTYRE

RECIPES

A Note on the Recipes

Executive Chef Christopher Brooks chose the recipes in this book with the resources and needs of the home cook in mind. There's a world of difference between the wherewithal of professional kitchens such as the one he presides over at Blantyre and even the most well-equipped of domestic kitchens. As he explains, "You have more things on hand in a professional kitchen — things like stocks and dressings, vegetables and herbs already peeled and chopped. But at home if a recipe calls for stock, you have to make it first. You have to do all the vegetables. Then you have to wash the dishes. At work we don't have to do that. Well . . . not often!"

Add these practical advantages to the refined technical skills that professional cooks bring to their work, their stoves and equipment, and their access to rare ingredients, and some of the dishes that professionals make can be difficult or impossible to reproduce in a domestic kitchen. Fortunately, a lot are not. Christopher points out, "Many of my recipes that we make at Blantyre can be done at home. I wanted to feature these rather than those that call on special resources so this book would appeal to a wider range of people. I always emphasize simplicity: the best ingredients cooked well."

Reflecting his emphasis on simplicity and seasonal cooking, the recipes are arranged by *Winter, Spring, Summer,* and *Fall* selections, plus sections on *Canapés* and *Breakfast.* Among them are guests' favorites from Blantyre's menus. From Breakfast comes Mango Lassi and the chunky marmalade and dark berry jam that everyone loves to spread on toast or pastries. (The recipes are on pages 221, 230, and 229 respectively.) From the Winter Barbecue menu there's Scotch Toddy Marinated Beef Tenderloin (recipe on page 144); the Spring section offers Cape Diver Scallops with Crushed Avocado and Citrus Salad — Christopher's favorite because "it just talks fresh and light." (The recipe is on page 158). Look for the recipe for Cobb Salad from Blantyre's lunch menu on page 180 in the Summer section and for the recipe for Christopher's wonderful Sticky Toffee Pudding on page 216 in the Fall section.

Chef de Cuisine Arnaud Cotar

The overture to dinner at Blantyre is canapés — "little bites of Paradise," as Chef Christopher Brooks calls them. These enticing morsels change every night but may include miniature asparagus flans, tiny lamb brochettes, baby Yorkshire puddings topped with roast beef and horseradish, or warm gougères, fresh from the oven and redolent of cheese. These alluring mouthfuls promise the symphony of tastes to come at the dinner table, and nothing complements the hopeful anticipation better than Champagne. Try Krug, Louis Roederer or Roederer Estate L'Hermitage to set a sparkling tone for the evening.

Christelle Cotar, Blantyre's Wine Director, also suggests "bubbles from around the world," and for those who prefer a white wine, a Viognier, a Chenin Blanc, or a Vouvray from Hüet.

CANAPÉS

ASPARAGUS FLAN

These miniature flans capture the very essence of asparagus.

1 bunch asparagus (about 1 pound)	*1 egg plus 1 egg yolk*
3/4 cup heavy cream	*Salt and pepper to taste*
1/4 cup milk	

Preheat the oven to 325 degrees, and lightly grease 8 demitasse cups with butter.

Wash the asparagus, and trim off the woody ends. Slice the asparagus thinly, and put in a heavy-bottomed saucepan with the cream and milk. Bring to simmering over medium heat. Cook for about 5 minutes or until the asparagus is tender.

Tip into a blender, and blend until smooth. Add the egg and the additional yolk, and blend until thoroughly mixed. Season to taste with salt and pepper.

Pour slightly less than 1/4 cup of the mixture into each prepared cup. Set the cups in a shallow baking dish, and fill the dish with water halfway up the sides of the cups. Bake for around 15 minutes or until the surface is dry and slightly domed in the center. Test for doneness by slipping a knife blade in the middle. It comes out clean when the flan is ready. Serve warm or at room temperature.

Serves 8

Tiny canapés entice the palate before dinner. Seen here from left to right: an Asparagus Flan (recipe opposite), a Petite Gougère (recipe page 110), and a Lamb Brochette with Lemon Aioli (recipe page 111).

PETITES GOUGÈRES

Gougère is a classic dish of Burgundy in France,
traditionally made as a great cheesy puff. These tiny gougères
are served before dinner. If you have made profiteroles
or any other choux pastry confection, you will
recognize gougères as their savory cousins.

1/2 milk	*Dash cayenne pepper*
1/2 cup water	*2 cups all-purpose flour*
6 tablespoons butter	*2 eggs, lightly beaten*
Salt to taste	*2 cups grated Gruyere cheese*

Preheat the oven to 375 degrees, and line 2 baking sheets with parchment paper.

Put the milk, water, butter, salt, and cayenne into a medium saucepan, and heat over a moderate burner until the butter melts.

Remove from the heat. Dump in all the flour, and stir it vigorously. It will make a pale, sticky mass. Return to the heat, and stir for about half a minute; then transfer to the bowl of a food processor. Let the mixture cool for 3 to 4 minutes. Then add the beaten eggs one at a time. Process for about 15 seconds after each egg is added.

Reserve about a tablespoon of the cheese. Add the rest to the slightly warm mixture, and stir just until it is combined. Using a piping bag or a teaspoon, shape walnut-sized dollops of the mixture on the parchment paper. Sprinkle a few shreds of the reserved cheese on each one

Bake for 10 to 12 minutes or until the surface is a friendly golden-brown and the gougères smell deliciously cheesy. Serve warm from the oven.

Makes 24 to 30 gougères

LAMB BROCHETTES *with* LEMON AIOLI

Grilling brings out the best flavors in lamb. These little skewers of lamb evoke all the scents and delights of a Mediterranean summer.

For the lemon aioli

1/2 cup mayonnaise

Zest of 1 lemon

1/2 teaspoon mashed garlic

1 teaspoon finely chopped fresh parsley

Salt and pepper to taste

For the lamb brochettes

1 pound lamb loin, cut into 1/2-inch cubes

1 medium zucchini, cut into 1/2 inch cubes

1 red pepper, cut into 1/2 inch cubes

Salt and pepper to taste

To make the lemon aioli, mix the mayonnaise, lemon zest, garlic and parsley together. Season to taste with salt and pepper, and keep in the fridge until ready to use.

To make the lamb brochettes, soak 5-inch brochette sticks in water for about 20 minutes. Thread the lamb and vegetables on the sticks in this order: lamb, zucchini, lamb, pepper, lamb. Sprinkle with salt and pepper to taste.

To cook, preheat the broiler until very hot. Put the brochettes on a rack set over a roasting pan, and broil, turning once, until cooked through. This takes about 4 to 6 minutes, depending on whether you like the lamb pink in the center or cooked thoroughly.

Makes about 15 brochettes

LOBSTER *and* CHIPOTLE SALAD

What could be simpler or more delicious than this lobster salad?
Serve it on teaspoons as a canapé. Or for special occasions,
multiply the quantities, and serve it as a first course
on a bed of lettuce or mesclun.

1/2 pound lobster meat, diced

1 scallion, sliced into thin disks

4 tablespoons mayonnaise

1/4 teaspoon diced chipotle pepper in adobo sauce

1/2 teaspoon grated lime zest

1/2 teaspoon chopped cilantro

Thoroughly mix the lobster, scallion, mayonnaise, chipotle pepper, lime zest, and cilantro. Serve on teaspoons.

Makes 16 canapés

SMOKED-SALMON ROULADES

These pretty smoked-salmon pinwheels always appeal.
Be sure to use thinly sliced bread that rolls up easily.

*8 square slices of whole-wheat bread,
each 4 to 5 inches square*

4 tablespoons soft cream cheese

Zest of 1/2 lemon

1/2 teaspoon chopped dill

4 to 6 ounces sliced smoked salmon

Choose bread that is fresh and not crumbly. Cut off the crusts. Mash the cream cheese with the lemon zest and dill, and spread evenly on the bread.

Arrange slices of smoked salmon on top of the cream cheese. With scissors, snip off any salmon that hangs over the edges. Roll up the bread into a sausage shape, and wrap tightly in plastic wrap. Put in the fridge for at least two hours. (If some cracks appear in the bread as you roll it, don't worry: The tight wrapping and the rest in the fridge will smooth them out.)

To serve, cut each roll-up into 1-inch disks using a saw-edged knife.

Makes 16 canapés

YORKSHIRE PUDDING *with* ROAST BEEF
AND HORSERADISH CREAM

With this canapé, Chef Christopher Brooks has turned
England's favorite Sunday lunch into a pre-dinner
foretaste of the delights to come.

For the Yorkshire pudding

1 cup all-purpose flour

1/4 teaspoon salt

3 eggs

1/3 cup milk

1/3 cup water

Oil for greasing the pans

For the roast beef and horseradish

10- to12-ounce New York strip loin steak

Salt and black pepper to taste

1 tablespoon olive oil

2 tablespoons horseradish

2 tablespoons sour cream, or more to taste

To make the Yorkshire pudding batter, mix the flour and salt in a large mixing bowl. Make a well in the center, and add the eggs, milk, and water. Stir to combine. Then whisk briskly for at least 5 minutes or until the mixture is full of bubbles. Let stand for at least an hour — overnight if possible.

To make the roast beef, preheat the oven to 400 degrees. Season the steak with salt and pepper, and brush with the olive oil. Heat a nonstick frying pan over high heat. When hot, sear the steak for about a minute on each side or until the surface looks handsomely brown. Transfer the meat to the oven, and roast until it reaches an internal temperature of 140 degrees on an instant-read thermometer. This takes about 8 minutes, less if you want the meat rare. Remove, cover, and let rest while you bake the Yorkshire puddings.

To bake the Yorkshire puddings, increase the oven temperature to 425 degrees. Oil the cups of a mini-muffin pan or small tartlet pans. (The cup capacity should be about 1/8 cup.) Place the unfilled pan in the hot oven for 3 to 4 minutes to heat. Pour about 1 tablespoon of the batter into each cup. They should be just half full. Return the pan quickly to the oven, and bake for 8 to 10 minutes or until the puddings are golden and puffed. Cool on a rack.

While the puddings are cooling, mix the horseradish with the sour cream, and thinly slice the beef.

To assemble, put about 1/4 teaspoon of the horseradish in the center of each Yorkshire Pudding — they collapse as they cool, leaving a convenient hollow — and top with a slice of roast beef.

Makes about 24 canapés

Canapés before dinner hint at the pleasures to come. Here from left to right is a Yorkshire Pudding with Roast Beef and Horseradish (recipe page 113), a Smoked Salmon Roulade (recipe page 112), Seared Tuna with Mango-Onion Relish (recipe opposite), and a spoonful of elegant Lobster and Chipotle Salad (recipe page 112).

SEARED TUNA *with* MANGO-ONION RELISH

The sweetly tart relish partners perfectly with cubes of tuna.
Any leftover relish is good on sandwiches or with cold cuts.

For the mango-onion relish

1 onion, quartered and thinly sliced

3 tablespoons cider vinegar

1 tablespoon dark-brown sugar

1 sprig thyme

1/2 bay leaf

Salt and pepper to taste

For the seared tuna

1 pound 1-inch-thick tuna

2 tablespoons olive oil

1/2 mango, finely diced

1/4 cup mango-onion relish

1/4 teaspoon cilantro

To make the relish, put the sliced onion in a small saucepan with the vinegar, sugar, thyme and bay leaf. Add a little salt and pepper to taste; cover the pan, and cook gently over low heat until the onion is very soft and the liquid has evaporated.

To prepare the tuna, cut into 1-inch wide sticks. Heat the oil in a frying pan over high heat, and cook the tuna for 1 to 2 minutes on each of the four sides of the squares. Remove to a cutting board, and cut each stick into 1/2-inch slices. The result will be little bricks of tuna, which should still be pink in the center.

Mix the mango, onion relish, and cilantro. Dollop the mixture on each piece of tuna, and serve. (Cover any leftover relish with plastic wrap, and store in the fridge.)

Makes about 15 canapés

BLANTYRE WINTER

WINTER MENU

Celeriac soup
123

Twice baked cheese soufflés
135

Winter greens with blue cheese beignets,
toasted pecans and a pear dressing
128

Beef stew
140

Steamed pear sponge pudding
150

When Berkshire cottages like Blantyre were in their Gilded Age heyday, oysters were popular with all classes of society because the New York and New England coasts had plentiful supplies. They reached Lenox and Stockbridge in prime condition via the frequent train service. Oysters are rarer and more of a luxury today, but Massachusetts waters still produce deliciously briny specimens, with Duxbury oysters being special favorites at Blantyre. They often star at winter barbecues, and skating servers deliver trays of them to the ice rink, each oyster perched on its very own snowball.

At home, a traditional oyster plate with hollows will nest the oyster and prevent them from wobbling and losing their juice. You can also serve oysters on a tray of crushed ice or seaweed. For a more vivid background, settle them on a tray of frozen cranberries.

OYSTERS *on* SNOWBALLS

1 dozen oysters
Tabasco or other hot sauce

Lemon halves
Melted butter

Wash the oysters under cold running water to remove any grit or mud. To open them, use a short, thick-bladed knife. Avoid using a very sharp knife; an old table knife is good. Wrap your hand in a kitchen towel, or wear a gardening glove. Holding the oyster in this hand, poke the tip of the knife in the hinge of the shell and work at it firmly but not savagely until it loosens. Then slide the knife across the oyster, keeping the blade flush with shell, cutting the muscle that holds the oyster. Do not wiggle the knife at this point because you don't want to cut the oyster itself. Be sure to hold it steadily so you don't lose the juice. Lift off the top shell, and remove any fragments that have fallen onto the oyster. Serve with the Tabasco and lemon halves and melted butter so guests can add what they like before swallowing their oyster.

Serves 1 to 6, depending on guests' appetite or oyster size

Wine Note: Oysters are at their best with a light white Chablis Premier Cru from Burgundy or a Muscadet from the Loire Valley.

CELERIAC SOUP

1 celeriac (about 1 3/4 to 2 pounds)

1 leek, white and pale-green part only,
   washed and sliced

1 10-inch celery stalk, diced

1 small clove garlic, chopped

1 medium onion, peeled and diced

1 bay leaf

6 cups water

1 teaspoon salt or to taste

1 cup light cream

Peel the celeriac, and cut into 1-inch cubes. You should have about 5 cups of celeriac cubes. Put them into a soup pan along with the leek, celery, garlic, onion, bay leaf, water, and salt to taste. Bring to a boil, and then simmer the vegetables for about 20 to 25 minutes or until they are all very tender.

Strain the mixture, reserving the liquid. Puree the vegetables in a food processor or through a food mill. Return to the pan, add the reserved liquid, and bring to simmering again. Stir in the cream, and then check for seasoning, adding more salt if you prefer it.

Serves 8

These appealing bunnies with jeweled ears are among Blantyre's collection of salt and pepper shakers.

Celeriac is one of Chef Christopher Brooks's favorite vegetables. "It can go with so much—nearly all meats and fish," he says, "and it can be cooked in so many ways: pureed, roasted, steamed, braised." In the center of a bowl of this soup he serves a juicy seared scallop or a scoop of lobster or crab salad bound with a touch of mayonnaise.

Winter's magic — helped by the hard work of Ron and Blantyre's ground crew — floods the tennis courts,
transforming them into a skating rink scintillating with light.

Guests can enjoy the fragrance of the pine garlands while sipping hot chocolate
topped with homemade marshmallows at the tables frozen in the ice, with chairs that conveniently glide.

Ripe Bartlett pears, greens from local Equinox Farm, fluffy beignets, and a little spice from the toasted pecans team up in a hearty, full-flavored salad that's perfect for winter.

WINTER GREENS *with* BLUE CHEESE BEIGNETS, TOASTED PECANS, *and* PEAR DRESSING

For the pecans
3/4 cup pecan halves
1 tablespoon vodka
1 teaspoon sugar
Dusting cayenne pepper

For the pear dressing
2 tablespoons sherry vinegar
8 tablespoons olive oil
Salt and pepper to taste
2 tablespoons diced ripe Bartlett pear

For the blue cheese beignets
6 ounces crumbled blue cheese

1/2 stick butter at room temperature
1/2 cup all-purpose flour
3 eggs, lightly beaten
Olive oil for frying

For the salad
1 large ripe Bartlett pear
1 head Belgium endive, leaves separated
1 bunch watercress, washed, picked
    over, and dried
2 cups mixed salad greens, washed
    and dried

To prepare the pecans, preheat the oven to 325 degrees. Toss the pecans first with the vodka, then the sugar and cayenne. Arrange in a single layer on a pie plate, and toast for 8 to 10 minutes or until fragrant and a shade or two darker. Watch them carefully during the last couple of minutes as they easily burn.

To prepare the dressing, mix the sherry vinegar with the oil. Add salt and pepper to taste and the diced pear.

To prepare the beignets, mash together the crumbled blue cheese and the butter in a bowl. Thoroughly stir in the flour, then mix in the eggs. Pour 2 inches of olive oil in a saucepan or deep frying pan, and set it over high heat. Scoop the mixture into small balls — you should get 14 to 16 of them from this quantity — and fry a few at a time in the hot oil. They pop to the surface after being in the oil for about 30 seconds — the underside browns in about 1 minute, and then you should flip them

over for the other side to brown, which takes only about 30 seconds. Drain on paper towels.

To prepare the salad, peel and thinly slice the pear. Put three slices on each serving plate. Dress the salad greens with the pear dressing and pile on top of the sliced pear. Arrange the pecans and blue cheese beignets around it.

Serves 6

After snowshoeing through the snowy landscape or skating across the tennis court ice rink, Blantyre guests can enjoy lush pots of Chef Christopher Brooks's creamy fondue — his version of the traditional Swiss dish.

FONDUE

1/2 cup dry white wine

1 1/2 cups plus 1/2 cup cream

1 tablespoon cornstarch

Salt and white pepper to taste

1 pound grated Gruyere cheese

Pinch cayenne pepper

6 warmed white-bread rolls

In a fondue pot or other heavy bottomed small saucepan over medium heat, boil the wine and then add the 1 1/2 cups of cream.

Mix the cornstarch to a thin paste with a tablespoon of water. Stir in a little of the hot cream, and then stir it into the mixture in the pan, and bring it back to the boil. Let it thicken, and then season to taste with salt and pepper.

Stir in the Gruyere, and simmer until the mixture is hot and smoothly blended. Season again with a pinch of cayenne. Consider the thickness of the mixture. If it is thicker than you like it, add the remaining 1/2 cup of cream.

Cut the warmed rolls into bite-size pieces, and put in a serving basket. Serve these with the fondue still in its pot. To spear the bread and dip it into the fondue, guests will need long fondue forks with wooden or plastic handles that don't conduct heat.

Serves 6

Snowshoeing to the swings

Snowshoeing on the upper terrace of Blantyre

TWICE-BAKED CHEESE SOUFFLÉS

3 tablespoons butter

3 tablespoons flour

1 cup whole milk, warmed

Salt and white pepper to taste

4 whole eggs separated plus 1 egg white

2 cups grated sharp Cheddar cheese

Prepare 4 soufflé dishes or ramekins, each of 1-cup capacity, by greasing them generously with butter. Preheat the oven to 400 degrees, and position a rack a little lower than center.

Melt the butter in a heavy saucepan over low heat. Remove from the burner, and stir the flour into the butter until you have a smooth mixture. It will be quite stiff. Return the pan to low heat, and stir in about 1/4 cup of the milk. As the milk mixes in, slowly add the remaining milk 1/4 cup at a time, stirring constantly. The mixture will smooth into a thick sauce. Stir it over very low heat for a few minutes.
With a fork or small whisk, thoroughly beat the 4 egg yolks, and then stir them into the sauce. Finally, stir in the cheese, and cook over low heat, stirring until you have a thick, smooth sauce.

Taste the mixture, and then add salt. The amount depends on the saltiness of the cheese and your own taste. Also season with white pepper. (Use seasonings generously at this point because adding the beaten egg whites next will dilute the taste.) Remove from the heat.

Whisk the 5 egg whites until they form soft peaks. Pile them on top of the cheese mixture, and quickly but gently fold them in, turning up the mixture from the bottom to the top with a wide spatula until the entire mixture looks spongy.

Gently spoon the mixture into the prepared dishes, and bake for 18 to 20 minutes or until puffed and deep gold on top. Serve immediately. Alternately, let cool and serve later. Soufflés deflate but will re-rise if reheated in a 450-degree oven.

Serves 4 to 6 if made in smaller dishes

Wine Note: With the cheese soufflés, serve a light Italian wine such as Chianti Rúfina, or Riserva "Nipozzano" from Marchesi de' Frescobaldi.

Ethereally light but cheesily intense, these soufflés taste divine right from the oven but can happily sit in the fridge for up to three days before being reheated in a hot oven. For a change from routine, Chef Christopher Brooks suggests adding some crispy bacon bits before cooking them. At Blantyre, applewood-smoked bacon is generally used for its flavor and texture.

Their botanical name is *Hippeastrum*, which translates as "horseman's star" or, more prettily, "knight's star." They bring their starry beauty to winter days, though we now know them better as amaryllis. For the holiday season every table in the Conservatory has its own lovely plant. Standing tall, undaunted by the cold outside, amaryllis add their warm colors to the cosy delights of Blantyre in winter.

CHICKEN POT PIE

For the chicken and vegetables

3 cups chicken stock

4 chicken skinless legs

3 stalks celery, 1 chopped and 2 cut into 1/4-inch slices

5 carrots, 2 sliced and 3 diced into 1/2-inch pieces

1/2 cup chopped onion

1/2 small rutabaga

2 leeks, white and tender green parts only, cleaned and cut into 1/2-inch slices

For the sauce

1/2 cup white wine

1 shallot, finely chopped

8 peppercorns

1 bay leaf

1/2 cup cream

Salt and pepper to taste

2 to 3 tablespoons chopped fresh parsley

For the pot pie

17.3-ounce package frozen puff pastry

1 egg

2 tablespoons milk

To prepare the chicken and vegetables, put the chicken stock in a large pan. Add the chicken legs, chopped celery, sliced carrots, and onion. Cover and simmer for 35 to 40 minutes or until the chicken and vegetables are tender. Strain the mixture, reserving all the liquid and the chicken. Discard the vegetables. Break the chicken up into bite-size pieces, and set aside.

Add the sliced celery, the diced carrots, the rutabaga, and the leeks to the reserved broth, and simmer gently for 10 to 15 minutes or until the vegetables are tender but not soft. Strain, reserve the broth, and set aside the vegetables

To make the sauce, in another small pan, simmer the white wine with the shallots, peppercorns, and bay leaf until about half the liquid has evaporated. Strain this into the reserved chicken and vegetable broth. Then return it to boiling point, and simmer until about one-quarter of its volume has evaporated. Add half the cream and continue simmering until the liquid is reduced to 2 cups. Stir in the reserved chicken pieces

and vegetables. Add the remaining cream. Taste and add a little salt and pepper if necessary. Stir in the chopped parsley.

    Divide the mixture into 6 large ramekins or other 1-cup baking dishes. Grease the rims of the dishes with butter and set aside. Preheat the oven to 425 degrees.

To make the pot pie, beat the egg and milk together; set aside. On a lightly floured surface and using a lightly floured rolling pin, roll out the pastry. Using one of the ramekins as your guide, cut the pastry into circles that are 1/2-inch larger than the top of the dish. (Having the pastry a little bigger than the top of the dish counteracts the shrinkage that occurs during baking.) Cover each dish with pastry, and then brush the surface lightly with the egg and milk wash. Make three cuts in the center of the pastry with a sharp knife to allow the steam to escape during baking. Put the dishes on a baking tray and bake for 15 to 20 minutes or until the pastry is puffed, crisp, and golden.

Serves 6

*Ever since Blantyre opened its doors to guests in 1981 the Agraria potpourri
in the lovely rose medallion bowl has been scenting the house with its orange-citrus aroma.*

Joe and Ruby

BEEF STEW

The secret of this extraordinarily flavorful stew is that Chef Christopher Brooks lets the beef imbibe flavor from the marinade for a full two days.

2 tablespoon olive oil

2 pounds chuck or braising steak, cut into cubes

2 celery sticks, cut into 1-inch pieces

1 medium onion, chopped

2 carrots, cut into 1-inch pieces

2 cloves garlic, chopped

1 leek, cut into 1/2-inch slices

8 black peppercorns

2 bay leaves

1 tablespoon chopped thyme

1 bottle hearty red wine such as a Cabernet Sauvignon or Merlot

2 cups veal stock or other meat stock

Salt and pepper to taste

24 pearl onions

8 ounces mushrooms

1 tablespoon butter

1 tablespoon chopped Italian parsley

Heat 1 tablespoon of the oil in a frying pan, and sear the meat for 4 to 5 minutes or until it is brown on the outside. Put the meat into a large ovenproof stew pan, and add the celery, onion, carrots, garlic, leek, peppercorns, bay leaves, thyme, and red wine. Refrigerate for 2 days.

When ready to cook, add the veal stock to the meat mixture, season lightly with salt and pepper to taste, put in the oven at 325 degrees, and let the stew gently cook for 3 to 4 hours or until the meat is tender. Remove the meat with a slotted spoon, and set aside. On the stovetop, heat the pan with all the liquid, and boil until about half the liquid evaporates, leaving a sauce thick enough to coat the meat.

Meanwhile, prepare the pearl onions. First, drop them whole in a pan of water. Let simmer for 2 minutes and remove. Rinse with cold water to cool them down. Cut off the stem end, press the other end slightly, and the onion will pop out of its skin. Put the peeled onions in a pan with enough water to cover and a pinch of salt, and simmer for 10 minutes or until tender.

Prepare the mushrooms by washing and trimming the stems. Halve them. Heat the remaining tablespoon of oil in a frying pan, and toss the mushrooms in the oil over fairly high heat to brown the edges while letting them lose their moisture.

To finish the stew, return the meat to the reduced sauce, and reheat. Stir in the pearl onions and mushrooms. Check the seasoning, and adjust with salt and pepper if necessary. Finally, stir in the butter to give the sauce a shine. Sprinkle with the parsley.

Serves 6 to 8

Wine Note: Complement the deep hearty flavors of this stew with a lively white wine such as a Riesling from New Zealand or a Sauvignon-Semillon blend such as Kongsgaard and Hatton's On the White Keys from California.

The lovely William Yeoward glasses and decanters grace all Blantyre's tables. For a close-up view of the goblet, turn to page 220, where it is shown filled with Mango Lassi, a favorite on Blantyre's breakfast menu. For a red wine alternative to the white wine suggested to complement the Beef Stew, the decanter could be filled with a Burgundy such as a Volnay En Chevret from Maison Louis Latour, or the sturdy Syrah from Kongsgaard Winery's Hudson Ranch Vineyard in California.

Dining Room

The Scotch whisky in this marinade recalls the history of Blantyre's Scottish creator, Robert Warden Paterson, and the Scottish name he gave his house. This steak wins accolades at Blantyre's Snow Barbecues, and it's just as tasty—and awfully easy to reproduce—when made in your kitchen.

SCOTCH TODDY MARINATED BEEF TENDERLOIN

1 miniature bottle Scotch whisky (50 ml size)
Zest and juice of 1 lemon
2 tablespoons honey
Pinch ground cloves

Pinch ground cinnamon
Pinch ground nutmeg
4 six-ounce tenderloin steaks
Salt and pepper to taste

To make the marinade, in a bowl lightly whisk together the whisky, lemon juice and zest, honey, cloves, cinnamon, and nutmeg.

Lay the steaks in a single layer in a shallow dish. Pour the marinade over them, and place in the fridge covered with plastic wrap. Leave for at least 6 hours, turning the steaks two to three times so that both sides get bathed in the marinade.

To cook the steaks, turn the broiler to the highest setting. Season both sides of the steak with salt and pepper, place them in a pan beneath the heating element, and broil until the outside is slightly charred. (Alternately, to barbecue them, grill 4 inches from ash-gray hot coals.)

Serves 4

Wine Note: Blantyre's experts recommend a good single-malt Scotch drunk neat and without ice. Three suggested possiblities are a 16-year-old Lagavulin, a 19-year-old Oban, or a 50-year-old Macallan — if you can find it.

LEMON CURD

2 2/3 cups sugar   *9 lemons*

2 sticks unsalted butter   *7 eggs*

Sterilize four small canning (Mason) jars by submerging them in a large pan (such as a pasta pan) filled with water. Put the metal lids in separately. Boil for 10 minutes and leave in the water until you are ready to use them.

Take a medium to large saucepan and a heatproof glass or ceramic bowl that can sit on the saucepan without wobbling. Put water in the pan to a depth slightly lower than the base of the bowl. From time to time during cooking, check the level of water and top it up if it's running low. Put the sugar and butter in the bowl, and set the pan over low to medium heat. When the butter melts, stir it into the sugar. Grate the zest from 5 of the lemons, and add it to the butter and sugar. Squeeze the juice from all the lemons, and stir it into the mixture.

Thoroughly beat the eggs. Pour them through a sieve into the mixture. Discard any white membrane that remains in the sieve as it may leave white flecks in the lemon curd. (These flecks are tasteless and harmless, but they mar the appearance.)

After the eggs are added, stir the mixture frequently. The bottom and sides thicken first, so stir them into the middle to set evenly. The lemon curd is ready when it coats the back of a wooden spoon and you can draw your finger through it without the edges joining back up. Lemon curd sets more as it cools down, so at this point it will still look somewhat runny. Remove the jars from the water, and dry them with a freshly laundered tea towel or paper towel. Pour the lemon curd into the jars, and store in the fridge.

You can adjust lemon curd to your own taste after all the ingredients have been added. Add the zest of an extra lemon for a more lemony flavor or a couple of tablespoons or so more sugar for sweetness. If it is too tart for your palate or you want it to be richer and smoother, add up to 1/2 stick of additional butter or 1 extra egg yolk.

Makes about 4 half-pint jars

Chef Christopher Brooks notes, "Lemon curd is very nice to have around. Use it to fill tartlets, fill layer cakes, or serve it with scones and tea or just on toasted brioche or English muffin." Lemon curd is also a pretty filling for thumbprint cookies. You can make it at any time of year, but lemons are a winter fruit, and lemon curd made with the new season's crop tastes more lemony—and nothing could be sunnier on a dark winter day than all those yellow ingredients: lemons, butter, eggs.

Those brown-spotted bananas that have lingered in your fruit bowl are perfect for this recipe: They pack lots of sweet banana flavor. Banana bread is a beloved staple on Blantyre's hot-chocolate menu. It's also great for breakfast or with a cup of tea or coffee.

BANANA BREAD

4 very ripe medium bananas

2 1/2 cups sugar

2 teaspoons baking soda

3 cups flour

1 cup (2 sticks) butter at room temperature

4 eggs

1/2 cup sour cream

2 teaspoons vanilla extract

1 cup broken walnuts (optional)

Preheat the oven to 350 degrees, and set a rack in the center. Thoroughly grease three 3-inch by 7-inch loaf pans or two 9-inch by 5-inch loaf pans, and line the bottoms with parchment paper.

Mash the bananas with a fork, sprinkling them as you go with 2 teaspoons of the sugar. (The sugar helps develop the flavor.) Set aside. Mix the baking soda with the flour, and set aside.

In a large mixing bowl, cream the butter and sugar until pale and fluffy. Mix in the eggs one at a time, adding 1 tablespoon of the flour mixture with each one. Mix in the sour cream and vanilla extract and then the remaining flour mixture. When thoroughly blended, stir in the mashed bananas and the walnuts if you're using them.

Turn the batter into the prepared pans, and bake. In 3-inch by 7-inch pans, the banana bread will take 30 to 40 minutes to bake. Larger pans will take 50 to 60 minutes. To test for doneness, poke a skewer into the center; when it comes out clean, the banana bread is ready. Cool in the pans on a wire rack for 15 to 20 minutes; then remove from the pans to finish cooling.   Makes 3 small or 2 large loaves

HOT CHOCOLATE *with* HOMEMADE MARSHMALLOWS

For the marshmallows

1/4 cup cornstarch

1/3 cup confectioners' sugar

2 egg whites

1 envelope unflavored gelatin

1/2 cup hot water

1 cup superfine (bar) sugar

1 tablespoon light corn syrup

1/2 teaspoon vanilla extract

For each cup of hot chocolate

1/3 cup grated chocolate

1 cup milk

To make the marshmallows, first sift the cornstarch and confectioners' sugar together. Grease an 8-inch-square pan with a flavorless oil such as canola. Line the bottom with parchment paper. Alternately, add a tablespoon of the cornstarch mixture to the pan, and toss it around so that the pan is thoroughly coated. Set aside.

Whisk the egg whites in the bowl of an electric mixer until they form stiff peaks.

Pour 1/4 cup of the hot water into a small bowl, and sprinkle the gelatin on top. Stir and leave in a warm spot until the gelatin has dissolved. It will look clear rather than grainy. If it sets, simply reheat it by standing it in a dish of hot water.

In a medium frying pan with a heavy base, mix the remaining 1/4 cup of water and the superfine sugar. Heat over a medium heat, and stir until the sugar begins to dissolve. When the water looks completely clear, stir in the corn syrup, the liquified gelatin, and the vanilla extract; it will be a creamy white color. Now, with the electric mixer running, pour this mixture into the egg whites, and beat for another 15 minutes or until the mixture is pure white and very stiff. Turn it into the prepared pan, smooth it out as best you can with a spatula, and sift about 1 tablespoon of the cornstarch mixture on top. Let it set for about 2 hours.

Sprinkle the remaining cornstarch mixture on a clean cutting board. Using a wet knife, cut the marshmallow mixture into 2-inch squares, and ease them out of the pan onto the cutting board. Cut each square into four equally sized pieces, and toss them in the cornstarch mixture until they are dusted on all sides. Let them sit on a wire cooling rack or something similar to dry out for another couple of hours. Store in an airtight container.

Makes 64 marshmallows

To make the hot chocolate, put the chocolate and milk in a saucepan and heat over medium heat, stirring or whisking to blend. Then drop in some marshmallows. Serve with sliced banana bread (recipe opposite).

Makes 1 cup

Today, marshmallows are generally rubbery blobs that come in plastic bags. They can be fun, but definitely not gourmet fare. At Blantyre they are home-made. What a difference! These vanilla-scented morsels melt on the tongue as gently as snowflakes. Even those who shudder at the thought of mass-produced marshmallows swoon over Blantyre's, and the good news is that they are not hard to make at home. Children have a terrific time helping with the final dusting of cornstarch and confectioners' sugar.

At Blantyre, the comforting warmth of old-fashioned sponge puddings is enhanced by the enticing flavor of ripe pears and aromatic maple syrup from Tyringham, Massachusetts. The puddings are often served with chocolate ice cream—a reminder of the classic French combination of pears and chocolate in Poires Belle-Hélène.

STEAMED PEAR SPONGE PUDDING

1 1/3 cups all-purpose flour
1 teaspoon baking powder
1/2 teaspoon baking soda
6 tablespoons butter, room temperature
1/3 cup maple syrup, preferably Grade B

2 eggs
2 large pears, peeled, cored, and diced into 1/2-inch cubes
1 tablespoon Poire Williams

Preheat the oven to 350 degrees. Do not use the convection feature of your oven as it will dry out the puddings.

Thoroughly grease 6 half-cup ramekins or 6 foil cups with butter. In a bowl, thoroughly mix the flour with the baking powder and baking soda.

In a mixing bowl, cream the butter; then mix in the maple syrup and 2 tablespoons of the flour mixture. When this has blended, add another couple of tablespoons of the flour mixture and 1 of the eggs, and blend them in. Repeat this step. Finally, mix in the remaining flour, and fold in the pears and the Poire Williams.

Evenly spoon the mixture into the prepared ramekins. Set them in a baking dish and fill the dish with boiling water to come about halfway up the sides of the cups. Cover with tented aluminum foil, place in the center of the oven, and bake for 45 minutes. Check after about 30 minutes by poking a skewer into the center of the puddings. When it comes out clean, they are done.

Serve with chocolate ice cream.

Makes 6 puddings

Wine Note: Most Sauternes have orange notes, but Château Climens is more lemony. It's a perfect match for these puddings.

Main Hall Fireplace

BLANTYRE SPRING

SPRING MENU

Spring vegetable mélange
157

Cape diver scallops with crushed avocado and citrus salad
158

Rack of lamb with morels, peas and chickpea panisses
164

Pink grapefruit sorbet
169

Chocolate cloud cake
170

SPRING VEGETABLE MÉLANGE

6 baby carrots, scraped

6 baby turnips, peeled and halved
   (or left whole if tiny)

6 green asparagus, woody ends cut off

6 white asparagus, woody ends cut off

6 scallions, cut on the diagonal into
   1/2-inch pieces

6 ounces French green beans,
   ends trimmed off

3 tablespoons olive oil

1 green zucchini, diced into 1/2-inch
   squares

6 large morel mushrooms, chopped

Salt and pepper to taste

1 tablespoon aged sherry vinegar

1 tablespoon chopped chervil

Fill a large mixing bowl or a pasta pan with water and ice cubes. Bring a saucepan of lightly salted water to a boil. Blanch the carrots, turnips, asparagus, scallions, and green beans. Do each vegetable separately, cooking only until the crisp-tender stage, and then immediately drop the vegetables into the ice water. Carrots and turnips take about 5 minutes, green beans about 4 minutes, asparagus about 3 minutes, and scallions about 1 minute to cook.

Pour half the olive oil into a frying pan, and sauté the zucchini for 2 minutes or until crisp-tender. Remove and set aside. Sauté the morels in the same oil. Meanwhile, reheat all the blanched vegetables in a large pan of boiling water, salted to taste, for 2 minutes. Drain and arrange on a platter with the morels and zucchini. Season to taste with salt and pepper. Combine the remaining olive oil with the sherry vinegar, and trickle on top. Garnish with the chervil. Serve immediately.

Serves 6

Wine Note: Many countries make wines to partner with this dish. Choose a wonderful Grüner Veltliner from Austria, a Kabinett Riesling from Germany, a Sauvignon Blanc from South Africa, or a light Vouvray Sec, such as a Huët Clos du Bourg, from the Loire Valley of France.

Celebrate spring with a rainbow of baby vegetables, their flavor heightened by morels — one of the few mushrooms to appear in spring rather than fall. At Blantyre, eagle-eyed foragers can find them growing beneath old leaves in the woods in May. Also look for them between the rocks of dry stone walls or in old orchards. They can be hard to spot but enormously satisfying to find. You can also pick up these pointy-headed hollow mushrooms in specialty grocers and markets.

The marriage of vanilla and citrus is ideal for this spring dish. Its lightness and freshness make it a favorite with Chef Christopher Brooks, who notes that you can also enjoy the citrus salad with chicken instead of scallops.

CAPE DIVER SCALLOPS *with* CRUSHED AVOCADO *and* CITRUS SALAD

1 pink grapefruit

2 oranges

1 lemon

1 lime

1/2 teaspoon sugar

1/4 vanilla bean

1 large ripe avocado, peeled and pitted

Salt and pepper to taste

1 bunch watercress, washed
    and picked over

2 teaspoons olive oil

12 large diver scallops, dry

Over a bowl to catch the juice, peel the grapefruit, oranges, lemon, and lime. Cut the citrus into segments, making sure no pith or coarse membrane remains.

Take 2 to 3 tablespoons of the collected juice from the bowl, and combine with the sugar in a small saucepan. Scrape out the vanilla seeds from the bean, and add them to the mixture. Cook over moderate heat to make a syrup. Pour this over the citrus segments, and allow to cool in the fridge for 6 hours so the vanilla infuses the fruit.

Just before serving, crush the avocado with 2 tablespoons of the citrus salad juice, and season to taste with salt and pepper.

Heat the olive oil in a large frying pan over high heat. When it shimmers, add the scallops. Let sear without moving them for 2 to 3 minutes or until a deep, golden brown. Turn and sear the other side for 2 to 3 minutes until golden.

While the scallops are cooking, assemble the salad by placing some crushed avocado in the center of 4 plates. Top with the citrus salad and then the watercress. Finally, add the scallops. Serve immediately.

Serves 4 to 6

Wine Note: Blantyre's wine experts recommend the splendid Corton Charlemagne from Louis Latour of Burgundy to drink with this salad. Other good choices include Chardonnays such as those from Maté's Vineyard in New Zealand's Kumeu River region or the Leeuwin Estate Art Series from the Margaret River in Australia.

The mushroomy-gingery broth with its hint of cilantro makes this dish of crisp vegetables and shrimp deliciously refreshing — with not a lot of calories for anyone who's counting.

You can use purchased cooked shrimp for this dish. To use shell-on raw shrimp, peel them by holding the tail and pulling to remove the shell. You will see a black vein that looks like a pencil line running along the length of the shrimp. Strip this vein out and discard it using the tip of a sharp knife. Cook the shrimp by dropping them into a pan of boiling salted water. Let them simmer for 3 minutes or until pink and opaque rather than translucent.

SHRIMP IN DASHI

For the dashi broth
3 shiitake mushrooms, sliced
2 scallions, sliced into 1/2-inch pieces
1-inch cube fresh ginger, peeled and
   chopped
1/2 stalk lemon grass, chopped
1 teaspoon dark-brown sugar
1/2 sheet nori, torn into 3 or 4 pieces
1 quart water

3 tablespoons soy sauce

For the shrimp
1 small head Napa cabbage, thinly sliced
6 scallions, thinly sliced
2 carrots, grated
Salt and pepper to taste
2 tablespoons chopped cilantro
36 large shrimp, peeled and cooked

To make the dashi, put the mushrooms, scallions, ginger, lemon grass, sugar, and nori in a saucepan. Add the water and soy sauce. Simmer for 15 minutes. Cool and put in the fridge. Leave for 2 days to infuse.

For the shrimp, toss the raw Napa cabbage, scallions, and carrots together. Season to taste with salt and pepper, and place portions in 6 deep bowls or soup plates. Sprinkle with cilantro, and then place 6 shrimp on top.

Strain the dashi broth, and discard the mushrooms, ginger, and other flavorings. Bring the strained broth to the boil, and pour it immediately over the shrimp and vegetables. Serve right away.

Serves 6

TAGLIATELLE *with* PEAS, FAVAS, MINT, *and* PARMESAN

3 quarts water

Salt to taste

1 shallot, finely chopped

1 clove garlic, finely chopped

1/2 cup white wine

1/4 cup heavy cream

Pepper to taste

1 pound tagliatelle, preferably home
made or fresh

1/2 cup cooked green peas

1/2 cup cooked fava or broad beans

2 cups freshly grated Parmesan,
loosely packed

2 tablespoons chopped fresh mint

Everybody is enchanted by the pretty jeweled birds that hold salt and pepper for Blantyre's guests.

Put 3 quarts of water in a large pasta pan, and add a tablespoon of salt. While it is coming to a boil, prepare the sauce. Fresh or homemade pasta cooks in only 3 to 4 minutes, so begin the sauce before you put the tagliatelle in the boiling water.

To make the sauce, put the shallot and garlic in a saucepan with the wine, cover, and let them sweat until tender. Then uncover and boil until the wine is reduced to one-quarter. Stir in the cream, reheat, and let the mixture reduce by about one-fifth. Add salt and pepper to taste, taking into consideration that you will be adding Parmesan, which is a salty cheese, so little extra salt may be needed.

To cook the tagliatelle, drop it into the boiling salted water. Homemade or fresh tagliatelle will rise to the surface in about 3 minutes. Remove a piece and bite into it to make sure it is cooked through. (Dried tagliatelle takes about 9 to11 minutes to cook through. Check the package for cooking time.) When done, gently tip the pasta into a colander to drain. Return it to its pan to stay warm.

While the sauce and tagliatelle are cooking, reheat the cooked peas and fava beans in simmering water or in a microwave.

To assemble, pour the sauce over the pasta, and add the drained peas and fava beans. Toss gently over very low heat. Finally, add the mint and Parmesan, toss briefly again, check for seasoning, and serve.

Serves 4 to 6

Making your own tagliatelle is a labor of love, and it's worth it because its tender egginess is a perfect foil for peas, beans, Parmesan, and mint. It's time consuming work, so if you need to put a spring supper on the table fast, use fresh tagliatelle from the store. You can also use dried tagliatelle, but dried pasta typically takes about twice as long to cook as fresh.

Wine Note: The freshness, crispness, and minerality of a fine Soave Classico, such as Pieropan's La Rocca from Italy, make it a perfect pairing with this springtime dish.

From Blantyre's exquisite collection of glassware, the William Yeoward champagne flute stands on the left with an antique St. Louis gilded wine glass on the right.

Lamb, morels, and peas, all fragrant with the aromas of garlic and mint, are a classic combination on the spring menu. Morels can sometimes be found hiding under the leaves on Blantyre's wooded grounds.

Blantyre's herb garden

The panisses served by Chef Christopher Brooks with his Rack of Lamb are a specialty of Provence in the south of France. The chick-pea flour from which they are made gives them a slightly nutty taste. Lemon thyme, garlic, and chopped black olives add an additional layer of Mediterranean flavors. Indian cooks also use chick-pea flour, which they call besan, to make batter for coating fritters. Look for it in specialty groceries selling Indian or Mediterranean products.

RACK OF LAMB *with* MORELS, PEAS, *and* CHICKPEA PANISSES

For the mint hollandaise
2 egg yolks

1 tablespoon lemon juice

1 teaspoon water

1 1/4 sticks unsalted butter, cut into
    about 20 pieces

Salt and white pepper to taste

2 teaspoons (or more to taste) finely
chopped young mint leaves

For the chickpea panisse
1 1/4 cups chickpea flour (also called
    besan)

2 cups water

1 tablespoon olive oil

1/2 teaspoon chopped lemon thyme

1/4 clove garlic, crushed

Salt and pepper to taste

10 black olives, pitted and coarsely
    chopped

1/4 cup cornmeal

For the lamb
2 French-trimmed lamb racks

Salt and pepper to taste

2 small garlic cloves, sliced into
    thin strips

1/4 teaspoon rosemary leaves

3 tablespoons olive oil

1 tablespoon butter

4 ounces morels or baby bella mush-
    rooms, cleaned

1 cup blanched peas

To make the mint hollandaise, use a double boiler, or choose a heat-proof ceramic or glass bowl that will sit on the top of a saucepan without the bottom of the bowl touching the base of the pan. Fill the bottom of the double boiler or saucepan with a couple of inches of water, set it over low heat, and put the top of the double boiler or bowl on top. Add the egg yolks, lemon juice, and water, and whisk until the yolks thicken. Take care not to splash the yolks too much up the side of the bowl, where the heat could make them crusty and useless. When the mixture is hot and thick enough to coat the back of the spoon, stir in 1 piece of butter over very low heat. (Be sure to do this before the eggs get too hot and begin to scramble. Should they seem to be coagulating, quickly remove them from the heat, and whisk in a tablespoon of cold water until the mixture reconstitutes.) When the first piece of butter has been absorbed, add another. Continue in this way, keeping the heat low and stirring in the butter pieces one at a time until they are used up, and you have a thick sauce. Season the mixture with salt and white pepper. Taste and add more salt and pepper if needed plus a few drops more lemon juice if you want a tarter tang. Remove from the heat, and stir in the finely chopped mint.

To make the chickpea panisses, oil the base and sides of 8 four-ounce ramekins with olive oil. Sift the flour to remove any little lumps, and set aside.

In a medium saucepan, bring the water to the boil. When it's bubbling, add the olive oil, thyme, garlic, and salt and pepper to taste. As soon as the water returns to the boil, add the chickpea flour, whisking continuously so the mixture thickens into a smooth batter. This takes only a minute. (If by mischance the batter is lumpy, whiz it in a food processor to smooth it out.) Stir in the olives.

Divide the mixture between the 8 ramekins, patting the batter into the bottom and smoothing the tops. Let cool. (You can proceed to this point ahead of time and complete the cooking of the panisses when the lamb racks are in the oven.)

To finish the panisses, preheat the oven to 350 degrees, and line a baking sheet with parchment paper. Sprinkle the cornmeal on a plate. Unmold the panisses from the ramekins, and press each side into the cornmeal to lightly coat it. Sear them for a couple of minutes on each side in a lightly oiled nonstick pan. Remove to the baking sheet and bake for 5 minutes.

To make the lamb, rub the fat of the lamb racks with salt, and season lightly with pepper. Using the point of a sharp knife, make some incisions in the fat and into the meat; then stick in a sliver of garlic and rosemary leaves into each slit. Cover and let rest for 1 hour.

Preheat the oven to 400 degrees. Grease a roasting pan with olive oil. Trickle a little olive oil over the lamb. Bake for 25 minutes; then remove from the oven and let rest in a warm spot near the stove, covered with a cloth.

Heat the butter with a teaspoon of the olive oil in a frying pan. Toss in the mushrooms, season them lightly with salt, and sauté them for 4 to 5 minutes or until any liquid has evaporated and the mushrooms are browned and tender. During the last minute or so, toss in the peas. Season with salt and pepper to taste.

Serve the rack of lamb divided into chops with a panisse, some olives, and mushroom-pea mixture. Serve the mint hollandaise on the side.

Serves 4

Wine Note: This rich dish full of the flavors of southern Europe calls for a wine with tannin. Try a super-Tuscan from Italy such as Ornallaia, Sassicaia, or Tignanello. Other choices include Castel Giocondo Riserva, a Brunello di Montalcino from Marchesi de' Frescobaldi, or a Margaux from Château Lascombes from Bordeaux, France.

The classic French clafoutis comes with cherries, but variations are legion. In France, small plums or greengages find their way into clafoutis when they are in season, and Chef Christopher Brooks says that sliced ripe pears can be used in winter, when cherries are unavailable. For one of his savory versions of clafoutis, see the recipe with smoked salmon and leeks on page 204.

CHERRY CLAFOUTIS

1 1/2 cups halved and pitted fresh
cherries or 1 1/2 cups drained,
   canned imported Morello cherries
1/2 stick butter
1 cup ground almonds
1/4 cup all-purpose flour

3/4 cup sugar
3 eggs
4 egg yolks
1 1/2 cups milk
3/4 cup light cream

Preheat the oven to 350 degrees. Grease an 8-inch-square baking pan or a 9-inch deep-dish pie pan with some of the butter. Arrange the cherries in a single layer in the pan.

Melt the remaining butter in a frying pan over medium heat. Let it cook for about 2 minutes or until it turns a warm brown and has a rich nutty fragrance. Watch it carefully; it should not turn dark brown or scorch.

In a large bowl, mix the almonds, flour, and sugar. Make a well in the center. In a smaller bowl, lightly beat the whole eggs with the egg yolks and about 1/2 cup of the milk. Pour this mixture into the well in the flour, and gradually stir the flour into it. Add more milk as you go. When all the milk has been added, stir in the cream, and whisk thoroughly to make a smooth batter. Finally, mix in the browned butter.

Pour the mixture over the cherries, and bake in the center of the oven for 35 to 40 minutes or until a knife blade slid into the center comes out clean, and the surface of the clafoutis is very golden.

Cool on a wire rack for 15 to 25 minutes. Serve warm. For extra luxury, add a swirl of whipped cream or a small scoop of vanilla ice cream.

Serves 6

PINK GRAPEFRUIT SORBET

1 cup sugar   *1 cup pink grapefruit juice*

1 cup water

In a small saucepan, make a sorbet syrup by stirring together the sugar and water. Bring to a boil, stirring occasionally to make sure the sugar dissolves. Let cool completely.

Mix the syrup and the grapefruit juice together; then churn in a sorbet maker according to the manufacturer's recommendations.

Alternately, pour the mixture into a shallow dish and put it in the freezer. After about an hour or so, the edges will be frozen. Transfer the mixture to a food processor or blender. Process for a minute to break up the ice crystals, return it to the dish, and replace it in the freezer. Repeat this process two more times at roughly 45 to 60 minutes intervals, in each case processing before the sorbet is completely frozen. Finally, let the sorbet freeze entirely.

Serves 4 to 6 as a dessert, more when served as a palate cleanser.

Sorbets are a perfect light dessert at any time of year, and Blantyre offers a changing array of them. The enticing color and flavor of this pink grapefruit sorbet is perfect for spring — and for summer, too.

Top scoops of this pretty cooler with a bob of cherries when they are in season. A cluster of red currants, a couple of downy raspberries or a jaunty strawberry are other options.

Chocolate desserts can be dense, but this cloud of mousse on an airy sponge cake bed seems light enough to float away. The recipe comes from Chef Christopher Brooks's sister, who learned it from a pastry chef boyfriend. Its pedigree notwithstanding, this cake is easy to make. It needs to rest overnight or for at least 8 hours, so it's a good dessert to choose when you want something you can make ahead of time.

CHOCOLATE CLOUD CAKE

For the cake
1/4 cup sugar
2 eggs at room temperature
1/4 teaspoon vanilla extract
1/3 cup cake flour
2 tablespoons butter
1 ounce dark chocolate (72 percent cocoa butter)

1/8 cup Grand Marnier

For the chocolate cloud
3 cups heavy cream
1/2 cup sugar
1 1/3 cups cocoa powder
1 stick unsalted butter

To make the cake, preheat the oven to 350 degrees. Grease a 9-inch springform pan, and line the bottom with 2 sheets of parchment paper.

Warm the mixing bowl of an electric mixer by filling it with very hot water and letting it stand for a minute or so. Empty and dry it, and then put in the sugar, eggs, and vanilla. Mix to combine; then increase the speed, and beat for 10 minutes. The mixture should become pale, thick, foamy, and triple or quadruple in bulk.

While the batter is beating, melt the butter and chocolate in a small pan. Let cool to room temperature, but don't let it resolidify.

When the eggs and sugar are pale and very foamy, as described above, remove the bowl from the mixer stand. Sift in half of the flour, and fold it in with a spatula. Repeat this step with the remaining flour. Finally, fold in the chocolate mixture. When it is completely mixed in, gently pour the batter into the prepared springform pan, put it in the preheated oven, and place a sheet of heavy-duty aluminum foil lightly over the top to stop the surface from drying. Bake for 18 to 20 minutes or until the cake feels firm but springs back when gently pressed. Remove and let cool on a wire rack. Do not release the clasp on the pan or remove the cake.

To make the chocolate cloud, boil 1 cup of the heavy cream. Stir in the sugar and then the cocoa powder to make a smooth, thick paste.

Remove from the heat, and fold in the butter 1 tablespoon or so at a time. Stir until the paste is shiny. Let it cool down to 98.6°.

While the chocolate mixture is cooling, whip the remaining 2 cups of cream. When the cream is whipped, fold about one-third of the whipped cream into the chocolate mixture with a spatula. When it has blended in, thoroughly fold in another third, then the final third.

To finish the cake, soak it with the Grand Marnier, and then gently pour the chocolate cloud mixture on top. Cool in the fridge overnight or for at least 8 hours. Serve with espresso or a glass of Grand Marnier Centenaire.

Serves 8 to 10

Spring often arrives shyly in the Berkshires, hanging back then coming in meteorological fits and starts. Soon, though, balmy days paint the land with tender shades of green. It's too late for winter sports; too early for summer swimming, concerts, and theatre; but utterly perfect for tennis, croquet, and rural relaxation.

This eighteenth-century English dish was first known as Burnt Cream, which becomes Crème Brûlée when translated into French. It was a favorite of Trinity College in Cambridge, England, which earned it the alternate name Trinity Cream. Under any name, it's a favorite with Ann Fitzpatrick Brown's mother Jane, who founded Country Curtains with her husband Jack. Having tried it at lots and lots of restaurants, her verdict is "Blantyre's is best." The secret? Letting the vanilla beans sit in the mixture overnight to enrich the flavor. Also, be sure to cook it as slowly as possible so the cream stays satin-smooth.

CRÈME BRÛLÉE

2 vanilla beans

1/4 cup milk

2 cups heavy cream

5 egg yolks

3/4 cup superfine sugar

Put the vanilla beans in a heavy saucepan with the milk and cream, cover, and let simmer over very low heat for 2 minutes. Remove the beans, and set aside. Meanwhile, in a bowl whisk together the egg yolks and 1/2 cup of the sugar. Strain the milk over them, stirring continuously. Put the beans back in, cover the bowl with a lid or plastic wrap, and leave overnight in the fridge.

When ready to proceed, preheat the oven to 275 degrees. Remove the vanilla beans from the mixture, and split them lengthwise. Scrape out the tiny black seeds, and stir them into the cream. Pour the mixture into a shallow heatproof dish such as a gratin dish or into 6 smaller heatproof dishes, ideally no more than 1-inch tall, though 1/2-cup ramekins will do. Set the dish or dishes into a shallow pan or a roasting pan, and fill with water to come two-thirds of the way up the sides. Bake at 275 degrees for 1 hour. Put in the fridge to cool overnight or for at least 6 hours.

Just before serving time, turn the broiler as high as it will go, and heat it up for 10 minutes. Sprinkle the remaining sugar evenly over the crème, and place the dish or dishes on a baking sheet and run them under the broiler. Watch carefully as the heat caramelizes the sugar into a crisp golden surface, which takes 1 to 2 minutes. Do not let it get dark brown. Turn the dish or dishes as necessary to get as even a color as possible. Alternately, if you have a kitchen blow torch, you can caramelize the surface with it. Let cool before serving, or chill briefly if you prefer.

Serves 6

Wine Note: With this most luscious of desserts, you need the most luscious of wines — Sauternes. At Blantyre, it could be Château d'Yquem, Château de Fargues, Château Rieussec, or Château Suduiraut — or one of many more.

BLANTYRE SUMMER

SUMMER MENU

Vichysoisse
178

Salmon pastrami with cucumber panna cotta
185-186

New England cod with zucchini cake and romesco
188

Texas antelope with Georgia peach tatin and rosemary
190

Iced lime soufflé
194

It sounds superbly French, but actually Vichysoisse is a hybrid: part French, part American. Louis Diat, the French chef of New York's Ritz Carlton, invented it around 1917. He named it after Vichy in France. He grew up nearby, eating local leek-and-potato soups, but none is as creamy as Vichysoisse and none is served cold, two characteristics Diat identified by naming his soup *crème vichysoisse glacée.*

VICHYSSOISE

2 tablespoons butter	1/2 cup white wine
1 small onion, finely sliced	1 bay leaf
1 cup thinly sliced leeks, white parts only	3 1/2 cups water
Salt to taste	1 cup heavy cream
2 cups thinly sliced potatoes	2 tablespoons snipped chives

Melt the butter in a heavy-based saucepan set over medium heat. Add the onions and leeks, and lightly sprinkle with salt to taste. Cover, lower the heat, and let sweat until the vegetables are soft. Add the potatoes with the wine, bay leaf, and water, and bring to a boil. Then reduce the heat, simmering until the potatoes are soft.

Let cool a little, and then blend or process in batches until smooth. Season to taste, cool, and then chill in the fridge.

At serving, stir in the cream. Scatter chives on each serving.

Serves 6

ARUGULA AND ROMAINE SALAD *with* TOMATO-HORSERADISH DRESSING

4 tablespoons olive oil

1 shallot, finely chopped

1/4 teaspoon finely chopped garlic

1 cup peeled and diced tomatoes

1 1/2 teaspoons tomato paste

Salt and pepper to taste

2 basil leaves, chopped

1 sprig tarragon, chopped

1 teaspoon prepared horseradish

1 1/2 teaspoons sherry vinegar

1 romaine heart

8-ounce bag washed arugula

1 pint cherry tomatoes, halved

To make the dressing, warm a tablespoon of olive oil in a small pan over moderate heat, add the shallot and garlic, and cook gently, covered, until soft but not colored at all. Add the diced tomatoes and tomato paste, cover, and simmer gently until the tomatoes are soft. Transfer this mixture into a bowl, pressing it through a sieve to remove the tomato seeds. Add salt and pepper to taste plus the basil, tarragon, horseradish, and sherry vinegar. Whisk in the remaining olive oil, and check the seasoning, adjusting to taste if necessary.

Cut the romaine heart into 1-inch strips, and toss it with the arugula. Add the halved cherry tomatoes, toss everything with the dressing, and serve.

Serves 6 to 8

This salad doesn't lose its energy even on the hottest summer day because of the vivid flavors and varied textures of the sweet tomatoes, crisp romaine, piquant arugula, and peppery horseradish.

This early twentieth-century Minton soup plate, shown opposite, comes from a service for 16 that has been in use at Blantyre every night since 1981. Unbeknownst to Ann — and to her shock and horror — it was being regularly washed in the dishwasher.

Cobb Salad originated in The Brown Derby restaurant in Los Angeles in the 1930s when owner Robert Cobb chopped an avocado with tomatoes, celery, lettuce, and bacon strips. Later he developed the recipe by adding chicken breast, chives, hard-boiled egg, watercress, and Roquefort cheese. It was one of the first salads to be a main course rather than a side dish. It's Ann Fitzpatrick Brown's favorite lunchtime dish. To make it to perfection, Chef Christopher Brooks insists, "It has to be chopped like the classic — not shredded or julienned — and served with plenty of dressing to bring all the flavors together. It's great when the chicken and bacon are warm."

COBB SALAD *with* BALSAMIC DRESSING

For the dressing

1 cup olive oil

1/4 cup balsamic vinegar

1 teaspoon Dijon mustard

Salt and pepper to taste

For the salad

2 hearts romaine lettuce, washed and chopped

1 radicchio, washed and chopped

2 large cooked chicken breasts, diced

8 slices crisply cooked applewood-smoked bacon, diced

4 hard-boiled eggs, chopped

4 ounces (about 1 cup) crumbled blue cheese

1 large ripe avocado, diced

To make the dressing, put the olive oil, vinegar, and mustard in a screw-top jar. Secure the lid, and shake vigorously to blend the ingredients. (Alternately, whisk them together in a bowl). Season to taste with salt and pepper.

To make the salad, toss the romaine and radicchio in a large bowl. Add the diced chicken, bacon, eggs, and blue cheese, and toss again. Add the avocado last so it doesn't have time to discolor. Pour on dressing to taste, and toss once more. Save any leftover dressing in the fridge.

Serves 6

Wine Note: Choose a white wine like a light, crisp Sauvignon Blanc with citrus notes such as Cloudy Bay from New Zealand, or Ferrari-Carano or Spottswoode from California. An alternative is the Sancerre from Henri Bourgeois of the Loire Valley in France.

Salmon Pastrami (recipe on page 186) with Panna Cotta (recipe opposite)

The handsome berry basket from
Terra Firma Studios

CUCUMBER PANNA COTTA

1 envelope unflavored gelatin

1/3 cup hot water

1 tablespoon butter

1 small shallot, finely chopped

8 ounces unpeeled English cucumber,
  diced into 1/4-inch cubes

2 tablespoons chopped fresh dill

Salt to taste

1 teaspoon cider vinegar

1 tablespoon white wine

2 ounces (about 1/2 cup) peeled
  cucumber, thinly sliced

1 cup loosely packed baby spinach
  leaves

Finely grated zest and juice of 1 lemon

1/2 cup sour cream

Pepper to taste

Panna cotta is Italian for "cooked cream." Usually it is a creamily luscious dessert, but this savory cucumber version partners with the salmon pastrami, pictured on the opposite page. (The recipe follows on page 186.) It's just as good with smoked salmon. Intriguing to taste but simple to make, this is a lovely addition to many summer meals.

Put the gelatin powder in a cup or small bowl, and stir in the hot water, stirring until the mixture looks clear rather than grainy. Then set the cup in a dish, and pour hot water into the dish to surround the cup and keep the liquid warm. Should the gelatin show signs of setting, simply reheat it until it is liquid again.

Lightly grease with butter 8 small cups, such as ramekins or coffee cups. Set aside.

Melt the butter in a medium saucepan over low heat. Stir in the shallot and the cucumber. Season with a little salt, stir, cover, and sweat over low heat for 8 to10 minutes or until the cucumber has softened somewhat. Add the vinegar and wine to the saucepan, and let it simmer to reduce it a little. Now add the spinach, cook for another minute, and then tip the contents of the pan into a blender or food processor, and process it. While still warm, add the dissolved gelatin and the raw peeled cucumber, and process again. Add the lemon zest, and season to taste with lemon juice.

Strain the mixture through a sieve into a bowl. Do not force any solids through the sieve. Thoroughly stir in the sour cream. Taste for seasoning, and adjust to your taste with more lemon juice, salt, and pepper. While the mixture is still liquid, pour it into the prepared cups. Put in the fridge or other cool place for about 4 hours or until set. To unmold, run a thin knife blade between the panna cotta and the dish or cup. Invert each onto a serving plate, and give a sharp shake to release the panna cotta.

Serves 8

SALMON PASTRAMI

For the pickling spice
2 tablespoons black peppercorns
2 tablespoons mustard seed
2 tablespoons coriander seed
1 tablespoon hot chili flakes
1 tablespoon juniper berries
1/2 teaspoon grated nutmeg
1-inch piece cinnamon stick
6 bay leaves
1 teaspoon cloves
1 teaspoon ground ginger

For the wild salmon pastrami
5 ounces kosher salt
1 tablespoon honey
1 tablespoon sugar
4 teaspoons pickling spice
1 tablespoon pink salt
1/4 cup dark-brown sugar
1 clove garlic, minced
1 quart cold water
3-pound side wild salmon
2 tablespoons white peppercorns
2 tablespoons coriander seed

Pastrami made from salmon instead of beef? Perfect for summer! Serve it with cucumber panna cotta, or substitute it for beef pastrami for a lighter riff on the traditional Reuben sandwich. It's unlikely that the salmon Robert Warden Paterson shipped to Blantyre from his fishing trips to the Cascapedia River were made into pastrami, but anyone lucky enough to catch a salmon today will find this an intriguing way to prepare it. And, of course, the recipe is excellent for salmon from the supermarket.

To make the pickling spice, put all the ingredients into a spice grinder or a coffee grinder, and whiz them until they are blended into a coarse powder. (If you use a coffee grinder rather than a dedicated spice grinder, remove the coffee smell by first whizzing a couple of large cubes of stale bread in it. Remove the bread, and wipe the interior clean. If it still smells of coffee, repeat this step.) Store any leftover pickling spice in a lidded jar to use as a barbecue rub or for making pickles and relishes.

To prepare the salmon, put the salt, honey, sugar, pickling spice, pink salt, dark-brown sugar, and garlic in a saucepan with the water. Bring to the boiling point, simmer for 5 minutes, and then let it cool to room temperature. Put the salmon into a shallow dish such as a lasagna pan, and pour the cooled liquid over it so the salmon is completely immersed; if necessary, add a little more water. Refrigerate for 36 hours. Then remove the salmon, discard the liquid, and pat the fish dry.

Crush the white peppercorns and coriander seed together using a mortar and pestle or by whizzing them in a spice grinder until they are a

coarse powder. Press this mixture all over the top surface of the salmon. Leave it uncovered in the fridge until the surface is dry; then wrap in plastic wrap.

When ready to serve, slice thinly on the diagonal with a sharp knife as you would cut smoked salmon. Cover any unused portion with plastic wrap, and keep in the fridge.

Serves 12

Wine Note: A great white Burgundy such as Chassagne Montrachet from Domaine Ramonet or a Bourgogne Blanc from Domaine Leflaive balances the spice of this salmon.

Hammock between white pines beside the Conservatory

NEW ENGLAND COD *with* ZUCCHINI CAKE *and* ROMESCO

For the romesco

2 tablespoons olive oil

1 red pepper, finely diced

1 large ripe tomato, diced

1 shallot, diced

1 1/2 teaspoons tomato paste

6 saffron threads or a pinch of
    powdered saffron

4 basil leaves, torn

1 tablespoon chopped parsley

1 1/2 teaspoons thyme

1/2 cup water

For the zucchini cake

4 small to medium zucchini (about
    1/2 pound)

1 tablespoon chopped basil

1 tablespoon cornstarch

1 beaten egg

Salt and pepper to taste

For the cod

Salt to taste

1 to 2 tablespoons olive oil

6 cod steaks, about 1-inch thick

To make the romesco, heat the olive oil in a heavy-bottomed saucepan over medium heat. Add the red pepper, tomato, shallot, tomato paste, saffron, basil, parsley, and thyme. Stir, cover the pan, lower the heat, and let the vegetables gently sweat for about 5 minutes or until softened. Stir once or twice more. Add the water, and simmer until the peppers are soft. If the mixture begins to dry out, add a little more water. Puree and cool. The mixture should be thick when cool.

To make the zucchini cake, preheat the oven to 375 degrees, and lightly grease the side of a nonstick 8-inch layer cake pan or a dish of similar size. Lay in 2 sheets of parchment paper cut to fit the bottom.

Grate the zucchini on the large holes of a cheese grater. Put the grated zucchini in a bowl along with the basil. Stir in the cornstarch and the egg, and season to taste with salt and pepper.

Put the mixture in the prepared cake pan, and smooth the surface. Bake for 7 minutes and take out of the oven. Remove the cake from the pan by placing a dinner plate over the pan. Holding the pan and dinner plate together, invert the pan so the zucchini cake falls onto the plate. Remove the parchment paper from the top of the zucchini cake. Slide the zucchini cake back onto the second sheet of parchment paper in the pan, and bake for another 7 minutes.

To cook the cod, while the zucchini cake is in the oven, season it with salt. Heat the olive oil in a nonstick pan, and sauté the cod for 4 to 5 minutes on each side. To serve, cut the zucchini cake into 6 pieces, and place a cod steak on top of each piece. Spoon the room-temperature romesco on the cod.

Chef Christopher Brooks says, "Cod is often underestimated, but its mild flavor makes it a crowd-pleaser." That's especially true when it's served on an emerald zucchini cake with a scarlet splash of romesco. Christopher recommends a Caesar salad or a salad of baby greens with this dish.

Serves 6

Wine Note: A beautiful Chardonnay from California such as Kongsgaard, Kistler or Au Bon Climat tastes delicious with this dish. Or from Burgundy, you could choose the Meursault Premier Cru "Sous Le Dos D'Ane", Domaine Leflaive or a Puligny Montrachet.

*Christina's beautiful arrangment
of dahlias*

Christopher Brooks says,
"This dish is all about peaches:
ripe, ready, sweet." Low-fat
antelope makes this a lighter
game dish for summer. You
could use roast venison or
broiled venison chops instead
of antelope if you prefer.

TEXAS ANTELOPE *with* GEORGIA PEACH TATIN *and* ROSEMARY SAUCE

For the rosemary sauce
1 tablespoon olive oil
1 shallot, finely chopped
Salt to taste
1/3 cup port
1 tablespoon heavy cream
1 tablespoon crème de cassis
1 cup antelope or veal stock
1 large sprig rosemary
1 teaspoon butter

For the Georgia peach tatin
1/2 cup sugar

1 tablespoon water
1 teaspoon lemon thyme
3 Georgia peaches
17.3-ounce package frozen puff pastry

For the seared Texas antelope
4 tablespoons olive oil
Salt and pepper to taste
2-pound Texas antelope loin (or
    substitute venison)
Salt and pepper to taste

To make the sauce, put the olive oil in a small saucepan over low heat.
Stir in the shallot, season lightly with salt, cover, and gently cook for
about 5 minutes or until the shallot is tender. Stir in the port, cream,
and crème de cassis, and simmer gently for about 10 minutes or until
the mixture is syrupy. Add the meat stock and rosemary, and simmer
until the mixture is reduced by a half. Set aside while you prepare the tatin
and the antelope.

To make the Georgia peach tatin, you need a muffin pan with cups
that hold 1/2 cup of liquid. Have this pan at the ready while you make
the caramel. Layer the sugar evenly in a medium-sized frying pan.
Sprinkle with the water, and set over low heat. Gradually the sugar will
melt, at first looking clear and then turning golden. As necessary, use a
wooden spoon to move unmelted sugar into the melted part so that the
whole mass caramelizes together. After the sugar melts, it changes color
fast, rapidly becoming dark brown and tasting burned, so watch it carefully. As soon as it is pale gold, remove from the heat; it will continue to
darken quickly. At the deep-gold stage, pour it into 6 of the muffin cups.

Ideally, these should be neighboring ones because this makes it easier to remove the tatins when they are baked. You need only about 1/2 inch of caramel in the base of each cup. It will quickly harden. That's fine. Sprinkle it with the lemon thyme.

Set the muffin pan aside, and preheat the oven to 375 degrees. Peel the peaches: First make a crisscross cut across the stem end, and then put them in a large bowl, and pour boiling water over them. Let them sit for a minute or two; then remove and slip off the skins with a small paring knife. Cut each peach in half, starting your cut at the stem (rather than across the middle) so you end up with two curvaceous halves rather than having one side pitted by the stalk end. Discard the pit, and if the cavity has crusty red remains in it, scrape them out. (A melon baller is handy for this.) Put the peach halves in the caramel-lined cups, curved side down.

Defrost the frozen pastry according to the manufacturer's suggestions. Roll it out very lightly. Using a cookie cutter, cut out circles of pastry to fit the top of the muffin cups. Most muffin cups require 3-inch circles. Alternately, cut 3-inch squares of pastry with a knife. Fit the pastry over the top of the peaches, tucking any straggly bits inside. Bake for 20 to 25 minutes or until the pastry is crisp and deep golden. Remove from the oven and let stand for 5 to 10 minutes before unmolding. To do this, run a knife around the inside of each cup to free the pastry. Next, put a large plate or a cutting board over the top of the tatins. Holding both the muffin pan and the plate together, quickly invert and set down so the tatins fall onto the plate. There will be some caramel syrup, too, so don't do this until the tatins have cooled a little so you don't risk getting very hot caramel on your hands.

To cook the antelope, turn the oven up to 400 degrees, and with a tablespoon of the olive oil, grease a roasting pan or baking dish large enough for the meat. Season the antelope with salt and pepper. Brush well on all sides with some of the olive oil. Heat the remaining olive oil in a frying pan, and sear the antelope on all sides. Remove it to the prepared roasting pan, and roast for 20 minutes. Since antelope is a very lean meat, it should be cooked rare or medium rare because longer cooking toughens it. This is also true of venison. When cooked, let the meat rest, covered with a cloth kitchen towel, for 10 minutes before you carve it.

To serve, put a peach tatin on each plate. (If you have cooked them ahead of time you can reheat them in a 300-degree oven.) Set a portion of antelope alongside. Reheat the rosemary sauce, whisk the butter into it, and pour over the meat.

Serves 6

Wine Note: Choose a superb red Burgundy such as a Chambertin Grand Cru, Camille Giroud, or Armand Rousseau for this luscious combination of game and peaches.

PEACH *and* RASPBERRY SALAD

1/2 cup ruby port
1/2 cup red wine
1/4 cup sugar

3 ripe Georgia peaches, peeled
1 pint raspberries
2 teaspoons chopped mint

In a small saucepan, bring the port, wine, and sugar to a boil, stirring to dissolve the sugar. Let this syrup cool for 10 minutes.

Halve the peaches, and then cut each half into 4 slices. Pour the port syrup over the peaches. Add the raspberries and mint.

Leave the mixture in the fridge overnight. This looks rich and lovely served in wine glasses or goblets with a tiny scoop of orange sorbet.

Serves 6

Wine Note: For a wine as refreshing as the dessert, try a light Italian Moscato d'Asti.

Dark red, glowing gold: This salad has the warm colors of a Tintoretto or a Titian, yet it tastes delightfully cool and refreshing on a hot summer's day.

To make his iced-lime soufflé Chef Christopher Brooks uses the special kitchen tool shown here for grating the zest from the limes.

Like most neighboring Gilded Age mansions, Blantyre had an ice house where ice blocks cut from Laurel Lake in the depths of winter were stored for chilling summer food and drinks. Frozen desserts were among the most popular hot-weather treats in those pre-air-conditioning days. This iced-lime soufflé is all about velvety cream and tangy lime: simply magical — and few things are easier to conjure up. You can make it in individual dishes as in this recipe, or just simply pour the mixture into one large dish, and scoop out servings.

ICED-LIME SOUFFLE

12 key limes or 4 large ordinary limes   2 cups heavy cream
1 can sweetened condensed milk

Wrap parchment paper round the outsides of 6 four-ounce serving dishes (like ramekins) so it stands 1 inch higher than the rims. To do this, cut strips of the parchment 1 inch wider than the depth of the dish. Make snips on the bottom edge of the parchment to make it easier to wrap. Hold the parchment in place with a rubber band. This enables you to fill the dishes higher than the rim to give the effect of a risen soufflé.

Remove the zest from half the limes with a zester. Microwave all the limes, zested and unzested, for 20 to 30 seconds or until they feel warm but not hot. This breaks down the juice-bearing vessels inside so they yield more juice. Halve the microwaved limes, and squeeze the juice through a sieve (which will catch unwanted pulp and seeds). You should have 1/2 cup of juice.

Pour the condensed milk into the bowl of an electric mixer. Beat it for about 15 minutes or until it is very thick and white rather than cream colored.

While the condensed milk is being beaten, in another bowl, whip the heavy cream until it forms soft peaks.

Mix the lime juice and zest into the beaten condensed milk, and then fold in the whipped cream. Fill the prepared dishes with the mixture, letting it pile up beyond the rim and to the top of the parchment paper. Freeze for at least 6 hours or overnight. About 7 minutes before serving, remove from the freezer, and take off the parchment paper.

Serves 6

Wine Note: Eiswein is made only from grapes that have frozen overnight — hence the name, which means "ice wine." Freezing concentrates the natural sugars in the grapes, making eisweins lusciously sweet. Blantyre's wine experts favor Inniskillin Eiswein from Canada for a perfect pairing with this creamy dessert.

Covered Terrace

Chef Christopher Brooks uses coconut sorbet instead of whipped cream to bring tropical flavor and a touch of Arctic chill to the summeriness of the classic New England strawberry shortcake.

SHORTCAKE BISCUITS *with* STRAWBERRIES *and* COCONUT SORBET

For the coconut sorbet
1 cup sugar
1 cup water
1 cup canned coconut milk

For the shortcake biscuits
4 cups all-purpose flour
4 teaspoons baking powder

1/4 teaspoon salt
1/2 cup confectioners' sugar
1 1/2 sticks cold butter
2 eggs, beaten
1 cup milk
2 pints strawberries
1 to 2 tablespoons sugar (optional)

To make the sorbet syrup, heat the sugar and water in a pan, and stir until the sugar has dissolved. Bring to the boil, and then let cool.

To make the sorbet, thoroughly mix the sorbet syrup and the coconut milk. Process in an ice-cream maker according to the manufacturer's directions. If you don't have an ice-cream maker, pour the mixture into a shallow dish, and put it in the freezer. After an hour or so the edges will be frozen. Remove it and transfer the mixture to a food processor or blender. Process for a minute to break up the ice crystals, return it to the dish, and put back in the freezer. Repeat this process two more times at roughly 45-minute intervals, in each case processing just before freezing is complete. After processing for the third time, let the sorbet freeze entirely.

To make the shortcake biscuits, preheat the oven to 375 degrees, and either grease a large baking sheet or line it with parchment paper or a silicone mat.

Stir the flour, baking powder, salt, and confectioners' sugar together in a large bowl. Cut the butter into pieces, add to the bowl, and toss

them around with a fork. Rub them into the mixture.

Mix the eggs and milk. Make a well in the flour mixture; pour in the wet ingredients and gradually stir them in. Shape into biscuits about 2 1/2 inches in diameter by 1 inch high. Place on the prepared baking sheet, and bake for 18 to 20 minutes or until golden.

While the biscuits are baking, slice the strawberries, and toss with sugar if you want to sweeten them or make them juicy.

To serve, cut each biscuit in half, and spoon sliced strawberries on the bottom half. Add some coconut sorbet and replace the top half.

Serves 8 to 10

BLANTYRE AUTUMN

AUTUMN MENU

White-bean soup
204

Smoked salmon and leek clafoutis
204

Apple sorbet
219

Beef tenderloin with pommes pont-neuf and pepper brandy sauce
208

Sticky toffee pudding
216

Smoked ham or bacon gives this velvety bean soup another layer of woodsy flavor. For a vegetarian alternative, use mushrooms instead.

WHITE-BEAN SOUP

1 cup dried cannellini beans
1/2 onion, chopped
1/2 leek, chopped
1 celery stick, chopped
1 clove garlic, chopped
2 quarts water

2 ounces smoked ham or apple-
  smoked bacon, chopped into 1/2-
  inch pieces, or 2 ounces white
  button mushrooms, chopped
Salt and pepper to taste
1/2 cup heavy cream

Rinse the beans, and then soak in plenty of cold water overnight or for at least 8 hours.

When ready to cook, drain the beans and put them in a large pan with the onion, leek, celery, garlic, and the water. Simmer for 1 hour. Add the ham or bacon if using; alternately, add the chopped mushrooms. Continue simmering for about 1 more hour or until the beans are tender.

Let the mixture cool a little. Puree in batches in a blender or food processor. Return to the rinsed-out pan. Check the seasoning, and add salt and pepper to taste. Bring to simmering, and stir in the cream. Serve hot.

Serves 6

SMOKED SALMON *and* LEEK CLAFOUTIS

1/2 stick butter
2 leeks, white and tender green parts,
  cut in 1/4-inch disks
2 tablespoons water
1 1/4 cups all-purpose flour
1 tablespoon sugar
3 eggs
4 egg yolks

1 1/2 cups milk
3/4 cup light cream
4 ounces smoked salmon, cut into
  1/2-inch pieces
1 tablespoon chopped dill
Zest of 1 lemon
Salt and pepper to taste

Preheat the oven to 350 degrees.

Melt about 1/2 tablespoon of the butter in a small saucepan. Add the leeks, and stir to coat. Add the water. Cover and cook gently for 5 to 6 minutes or until tender.

Melt the remaining butter in a frying pan over medium heat. Cook for about 2 minutes or until the butter turns light brown and has a rich, nutty fragrance. Watch it carefully; it should not turn dark brown.

In a large bowl, mix the flour and sugar. In a smaller bowl, lightly beat the whole eggs with the egg yolks and about 1/2 cup of the milk. Make a well in the flour, pour in the egg mixture, and gradually stir the flour into it. Add more milk as you go. When all the milk has been added, stir in the cream, and whisk to make a smooth batter.

Use a little of the browned butter to thoroughly grease a 1-quart gratin dish or an 8-inch-square baking dish or a 9-inch deep-pie dish. Stir the remaining butter into the batter. Reserve one strip of the salmon to use later as garnish. Stir the rest of the salmon into the batter along with the dill, lemon zest, and salt and pepper to taste. Pour the mixture into the prepared pan, and bake for 35 to 40 minutes or until a knife blade slid into the center comes out clean and the surface is golden brown. Let stand for a few minutes before serving. Serve warm and garnish with the remaining salmon strip.

Serves 6 as an appetizer or lunch dish, 4 as a main dish

Wine Note: Balance the mixture of the rich and smoky flan with a Pinot Blanc, Pinot Gris, or Riesling from Domaine Zind Humbrecht or Hugel from Alsace, France.

Chef Christopher Brooks smokes Blantyre's salmon to ensure a fine, delicate flavor. In this variation of clafoutis — traditionally polka-dotted with cherries as in the recipe on page 166 — smoked salmon teams with leeks to make a savory dish. Serve it for lunch, as a first course, or for an at-home supper on a cool fall evening.

This is an elegant version of a perennial favorite: steak with fries. Leeks cooked this way — in a little butter and white wine — retain their shape and taste delicious. Try them also with lamb or with fish such as salmon, halibut, or cod.

BEEF TENDERLOIN *with* LEEKS, POMMES PONT-NEUF, *and* PEPPER BRANDY SAUCE

For the pommes pont-neuf
6 large Yukon Gold potatoes, peeled
Vegetable oil for frying
Salt to taste

For the leeks
2 large leeks
1 tablespoon butter
1/4 cup white wine
6 sprigs thyme

For the steaks and pepper-brandy sauce
6 six-ounce tenderloin steaks
Salt and pepper to taste
1 tablespoon olive oil
1 shallot, peeled and finely chopped
4 tablespoons brandy
1/4 cup veal or beef stock
1/4 cup heavy cream
1 tablespoon Dijon mustard
1/2 teaspoon coarsely ground black pepper
4 tablespoons cold butter, cut into 12 pieces

For the pommes pont-neuf, cut the potatoes into 2-inch by 1/2-inch lengths. In a deep fryer, heat the oil to 250 degrees. Drop in a few potato pieces (which will lower the temperature). Let the oil return to heat, and add more potatoes. Cook them all until they are tender and cooked through — test by poking with a fork — but still pale. Remove from the oil with a slotted spoon; season lightly with salt, and set aside.

For the leeks, peel off the coarse outer layers and dark-green tops. Make a 5-inch cut down from the top center of each leek, and then splay it out under cold running water to remove any soil trapped between the layers. Cut the leeks into 1/2-inch disks, and put into a saucepan with the butter, wine, and thyme. Cover and cook over low heat for 10 to 15 minutes or until the leeks are tender.

For the beef tenderloins, preheat the oven broiler to 500 degrees, and lightly grease a baking dish. Season the steaks on both sides with salt and pepper. Heat the olive oil in a frying pan, and sear the steaks on both sides. Transfer them to the baking dish and put under the broiler. For rare steaks,

broil for 2 1/2 minutes on each side; increase the time to 3 minutes per side for medium-rare, 3 1/2 minutes a side for medium, and 4 minutes per side for well done.

To make the sauce, add the shallot to the fat remaining in the pan used for the steaks, and let it soften over medium heat. Now pour in the brandy and let it sizzle for few seconds. Stir in the stock and cream, and cook over high heat for 2 minutes or until the mixture has reduced by one-quarter. Stir in the mustard and pepper. Add the butter 1 piece at a time, stirring each piece so it melts into the sauce before adding the next piece. When all the butter pieces have been stirred in, remove the sauce from the heat, but keep warm.

To assemble the dish, while you are working on the steak and sauce, turn the deep fryer up to 350 degrees. Cook the fries for about 2 minutes or until golden brown. At the same time, reheat the leeks if necessary. Finally, transfer the leeks onto warm plates, and place the steaks on top. Serve the sauce around the steaks, accompanied with the fries.

Serves 6

Wine Note: This dish needs a rich, full-bodied wine. Possibilities include a great Châteauneuf du Pape from Château de Beaucastel or Domaine du Vieux-Télégraphe. Alternatives include a Côte Rôtie from E. Guigal, or a fantastic Napa Valley Cabernet Sauvignon like Rudd, Chateau Montelena, Robert Mondavi Reserve, Joseph Phelps, or Far Niente.

Blantyre guests who request gluten-free meals can find many dishes on the menu to tempt them. This one is a favorite. Buckwheat — the flour traditionally used in Russian blini — is related to rhubarb. Unlike grass-family cereals such as wheat, buckwheat seeds lack gluten; for baking they are ground into a pale gray-brown flour. At Blantyre, pheasant breasts substitute for duck breasts when they are in season.

BUCKWHEAT CREPES *with* DUCK BREASTS, PARSNIPS, *and* WILD MUSHROOMS

For the mushrooms
2 tablespoons olive oil
1 pound mixed mushrooms, including
    some each of oyster, button,
    chanterelles, cremini, and black
    trumpet mushrooms
Salt and pepper to taste

For the parsnips
4 medium parsnips (about 1 pound)
    cut into 1/2-inch slices
1 cup milk (or more as needed)
1/4 teaspoon salt or to taste

1 tablespoon honey

For the duck breasts
6 duck breasts
Salt and pepper to taste
Olive oil

For the buckwheat crepes
1 cup pure buckwheat flour
Pinch salt
2 eggs, lightly beaten
1 1/2 cups milk
2 tablespoons butter

To cook the mushrooms, rinse them all quickly, then dry, removing excess water and dirt with paper towels. Chop them roughly. Heat the olive oil in a frying pan, add the mushrooms, and sauté for 4 to 5 minutes or until they are becoming tender and giving off their juices. Set aside to finish cooking later.

To prepare the parsnips, cut each half into 1/2-inch slices, and put them in a heavy saucepan with the milk and salt. Add a little more milk if needed to cover the parsnips. Simmer over low heat, stirring occasionally so the milk doesn't scorch on the bottom of the pan. Cook for about 20 minutes or until the parsnips are completely tender. Then add the honey, and mash the parsnips to a puree with the milk they cooked in. They should be like creamy mashed potatoes; add more milk if necessary to achieve this.

While the parsnips are cooking, sear the duck breasts. First, season with salt and pepper. Then with a sharp knife, make three or four slashes going through the fat but not into the meat. Grease a nonstick frying pan with a tiny amount of oil, put the pan on a moderately high burner, and place the duck breasts fat side down. Cook for 7 minutes over high heat so that a lot of fat runs out. When the fat side is an appetizing brown, flip over and cook the other side for 4 minutes for medium rare or 6 to 7 minutes to brown the meat all through. Transfer to a warmed dish, cover with a clean cloth, and let rest in a warm place for a few minutes.

As the parsnips and duck are cooking, make the crepes. Mix the buckwheat flour and salt in a large mixing bowl. Make a well in the center, and add the eggs and 1 cup of the milk. Stir together to form a batter, adding more milk if necessary to make it the consistency of heavy cream. In a small pan, melt the butter until it turns golden brown. For each crêpe, pour about 1/3 cup of batter into a lightly greased, 8-inch nonstick pan, tilting the pan to let it spread over the whole surface. Cook for 3 to 4 minutes or until the top surface looks dry; then flip and cook the other side for 1 to 2 minutes. Set the crepes on a warm plate, separated by sheets of parchment paper or foil. Keep them warm.

To serve, warm the dining plates. Return the mushrooms to the heat, and let them cook and sizzle for another couple of minutes. Reheat the parsnip puree either on top of the stove or in a microwave, and put some on each plate. Spoon a portion of mushrooms on half of each crepe, fold the other half over, and place the crepe on the parsnips. Position a duck breast on top.

Serves 6

Wine Note: A Riesling from Germany such as the slightly sweet Spätlese from Joh. Jos. Prüm or Dr. Loosen complements the duck in this dish. If you prefer a light red wine, try a Volnay Pinot Noir from Burgundy.

THANKSGIVING STUFFING

1 tablespoon butter	*8 ounces cooked chestnuts*
1 carrot, peeled and grated	*1 cup fresh breadcrumbs*
1 small onion, diced	*1 teaspoon rubbed sage*
1 stick celery, diced	*1 teaspoon dried thyme*
1 clove garlic, chopped	*1 teaspoon chopped fresh parsley*
Salt to taste	*1/4 cup Madeira*
1 pound sausage meat	*Pepper to taste*
1/4 pound chicken livers, diced	*3 eggs, lightly beaten*

Melt the butter in a small heavy-bottomed saucepan. Add the carrot, onion, celery, and garlic. Season lightly with salt. Cover and let the vegetables sweat over a low heat for about 5 minutes or until tender. If the vegetables stick to the pan, add a tablespoon or so of water, and stir before continuing to cook with the lid on the pan.

In a large bowl, combine the sausage meat, chicken livers, chestnuts, breadcrumbs, sage, thyme, and parsley. Pour in the Madeira, and mix well. Season to taste with salt and pepper, and stir in the eggs. To check the seasoning, make a 1-inch patty of the mixture, and fry it in a nonstick pan. Taste it when cooked through. If you think the mixture needs more salt and pepper, add it at this point.

Preheat the oven to 350 degrees. Grease a shallow 10 by 12-inch baking pan and put in the stuffing mixture. Alternately, form the mixture into a log roughly 9 inches long, wrap in greased aluminum foil, and put it on a baking sheet. Bake the stuffing for 1 hour and 15 minutes or until it is cooked through. Serve with turkey and cranberry sauce.

Serves 10 to 12

Thanksgiving dinner at Blantyre is cooked just as Grandma used to do, and this stuffing has become a must-have favorite. Dessert is always a buffet served in the Music Room, where guests while away the early evening listening to the piano.

Here's Blantyre's orange-flavored version of the essential crimson partner to the Thanksgiving turkey.

CRANBERRY SAUCE

12-ounce bag cranberries	*1 bay leaf*
1/2 cup sugar or to taste	*1/2 cup water*
Zest of 1 orange	*Salt and pepper to taste*

Rinse the cranberries and then put them in a saucepan with the sugar, orange zest, bay leaf, and water. Cover and cook over low heat until you hear the cranberries popping, and stir. Continue cooking, stirring often, for about 5 minutes or until you have a thick sauce. Taste, and add more sugar if necessary. Season with salt and pepper to taste.

Serves 10 to 12

Chef Christopher Brooks brought this pudding to America from his native England, where it is a big favorite. Here, too, it has become the first choice for many Blantyre guests.

STICKY TOFFEE PUDDING

For the cake	*1 1/2 cups sugar*
3 cups all-purpose flour	*4 eggs*
2 teaspoons baking powder	
8-ounce package chopped dates	
1 1/2 cups boiling water	*For the toffee sauce*
1 teaspoon baking soda	*2 cups dark-brown sugar*
2 sticks butter	*2 cups whipping cream*
	1/2 stick butter

To make the cake, preheat the oven to 350 degrees. Grease a 9-inch-square baking pan, and line the bottom with parchment paper. In a small bowl, mix the flour and baking powder.

Put the dates into a small saucepan, and pour on the boiling water. Simmer for 5 to 8 minutes or until completely soft. Stir in the baking soda, and let cool to room temperature.

In a large bowl or the bowl of an electric mixer, cream the butter and sugar until pale and fluffy. Mix in one of the eggs. When thoroughly blended, mix in a second egg with a tablespoon of the flour mixture. Add the remaining 2 eggs one at a time, adding 1 tablespoon of flour with

each and mixing well after each one. Thoroughly blend in the remaining flour mixture, and then gently mix in the dates and their liquid. Pour into the prepared pan. Bake in the center of the oven for 45 to 55 minutes. Test for readiness by poking a toothpick or skewer into the center. If it comes out clean, remove the cake from the oven.

To make the sauce, put the sugar, cream, and butter into a saucepan, and stir over gentle heat until the butter has melted and the sugar dissolved. Increase the heat and let simmer for a couple of minutes.

To serve, turn on the broiler. With a skewer, poke some holes in the warm cake, and pour over enough sauce to cover the top and run into the holes. Place the cake under the broiler, and watch it like a hawk to make sure it doesn't scorch; let it just sizzle. Cut into squares, and dish up immediately. Pour on more sauce — reheated if necessary. Offer the remaining sauce at the table. Serve with ice cream or whipped cream.

Serves 8

THIN APPLE TART *with* CRUMBLE TOPPING

For the crumble topping
1/2 cup flour
1/2 cup oatmeal
1/2 stick butter
1/2 cup sugar

For the apple tarts
3 apples, peeled, cored, and thinly
    sliced
1/2 stick butter, melted
1/3 cup dark-brown sugar
6 five-inch squares of thinly rolled
    puff pastry

Preheat the oven to 375 degrees, and line a baking sheet with parchment paper.

For the crumble, mix the flour and oatmeal in a bowl. Rub the butter into it so it looks like lumpy crumbs. Stir in the sugar.

For the tarts, lightly toss the apple slices with the butter, and then sprinkle with the brown sugar. Arrange the apples in the center of the

There's an elegance to having your own personal tart that makes Blantyre's apple tarts special, whether the apples are glazed, as is the tart in the picture, or crumble topped, as in the recipe on the right. Good apples for this tart include Cortlands, Northern Spies, Golden Delicious, and Granny Smiths for those who like a tart apple. McIntoshes are not good because the slices don't hold their shape in baking.

puff pastry squares. Crimp the edges of the pastry round the apples. Sprinkle the crumble on top. (You could also make the tarts in lightly greased 3-inch-diameter tartlet pans lined with 5-inch circles of pastry fitted into the pans. Trim off any excess pastry.)

Place in the oven, and bake for 20 minutes or until golden brown and fragrant. Let rest on a wire rack for a few minutes. Serve warm with vanilla ice cream.

Serves 8

Wine Note: The acidity of the apple pairs very well with the sweetness of Dolce Late Harvest from Nickel & Nickel of the Napa Valley, California. A Sauternes from Bordeaux or a Tokaji from Hungary are also excellent choices.

APPLE SORBET

1 cup sugar   1 cup apple cider

1 cup water

Combine the sugar and water in a saucepan, and bring to the boil, stirring occasionally until the sugar is completely dissolved and you have a syrup. Let it cool.

Mix the sorbet syrup and apple cider together. Churn in a sorbet maker according to the manufacturer's recommendations, or use the following alternate method. Pour the mixture into a shallow dish and put in the freezer. After about an hour the edges will be frozen. Transfer the mixture to a food processor or blender. Process for a minute to break up the ice crystals, put it back in the dish, and return to the freezer. Repeat this process two more times at roughly 45-minute intervals. Finally, let the sorbet freeze entirely.

Serves 4 to 6 as a dessert or more if served on the side with other desserts or as a palate cleanser between courses.

Cider was the everyday Massachusetts drink in earlier centuries, and many orchards still make it using several varieties of apples rather than just one, so their cider tastes intensely appley — the very essence of fall in New England. Hot cider with sugar cookies is served every afternoon throughout fall in Blantyre's Main Hall. Its flavor is captured in the recipe for Apple Sorbet — a light dessert that's perfect for autumn.

BREAKFAST

MANGO LASSI

*1 pound (1 or 2 large) very ripe
  mangoes*
1 quart low-fat natural plain yogurt

1/2 cup ice cubes
Splash of rum (optional)
6 well-shaped ripe strawberries, washed

Peel and dice the mangoes. Put the mangoes, yogurt, and ice cubes in a blender, adding a splash of rum if you like. Whiz on high speed until the mixture is thick and creamy. Pour into 6 goblets, filling each about three-quarters full. Cut the strawberries from the tip down toward the tuft of leaves, but don't cut all the way through. Anchor the strawberry on the rim of the glass, using the slit.

Serves 6

*A detail of the Dresden chandelier
in the Breakfast Room*

In India, mango lassi is a favorite way to fight brownout on a hot afternoon. On Blantyre's breakfast menu it's a deliciously healthful way to start the day — an alternative to juice or a creamy partner to the berry bowls. It arrives on the table enticingly served in William Yeoward glasses.

At Blantyre these pancakes are baked in rings and arrive on the breakfast table in a tower. Enriched with jewel-bright berries, lemon poppy-seed butter, and golden streams of maple syrup from the Curtin family of Tyringham, they are a Blantyre favorite. In winter, when berries are not at their best, roasted pears can replace the berries.

WHOLE-WHEAT BLUEBERRY PANCAKES *with* LEMON POPPY-SEED BUTTER

For the lemon poppy-seed butter
4 ounces (1 stick) unsalted butter at
    room temperature
Finely grated zest of 1 lemon
2 teaspoons poppy seeds
2 tablespoons confectioners' sugar

For the whole-wheat pancakes
1 1/2 cups all-purpose flour
1 cup whole-wheat flour

2 tablespoons sugar
1 tablespoon baking powder
1/2 teaspoon salt
2 cups milk, lightly beaten
2 egg yolks
4 ounces (1 stick) butter, melted
Finely grated zest and juice of 1 lemon
8 egg whites
Oil or butter for greasing the pan

To make the lemon poppy-seed butter, mash the butter with a fork; then add the lemon zest and poppy seeds. Mix in the confectioners' sugar until blended. Press into a bowl for serving, or chill for 1 hour in the fridge, and then form into a log for easy slicing.

To make the whole-wheat pancakes, mix together the all-purpose flour, whole-wheat flour, sugar, baking powder, and salt in a large bowl or the bowl of an electric mixer.

In a separate bowl, mix the milk and the egg yolks; then add the melted butter. Make a well in the center of the dry ingredients, and pour in the milk mixture. Add the lemon zest and juice, and stir to a smooth batter. Whisk the egg whites until they form soft peaks, and fold them into the batter.

Grease a pancake pan or frying pan with oil or butter, heat over medium heat, and spoon in the batter, using about 1/2 cup for each pancake. When tiny holes pit the surface of the pancake and the edges look dry — which takes about 4 minutes — flip it over and cook the other side, which takes only 2 to 3 minutes.

Serve the pancakes with a pat of the lemon poppy-seed butter and maple syrup. Leftover butter can be spread on scones — the recipe for them is on page 226 — or stored in the fridge or freezer.

Serves 6

The soft New England colors and country flavors of this parsley-speckled white omelet filled with woodsy mushrooms and creamy Vermont cheddar make it an appealing and satisfying breakfast dish. Baking rather than stove-top cooking ensures a trouble-free slide from pan to plate and a piping-hot arrival on the table.

EGG-WHITE OMELET *with* MUSHROOMS

1 teaspoon olive oil

2 to 3 tablespoons chopped mushrooms, preferably a mix of button mushrooms with oyster, cremini, and chanterelles

4 egg whites

1 teaspoon chopped parsley

2 tablespoons sharp Vermont cheddar

Preheat the oven to 375 degrees.

Heat the olive oil in a small pan, and sauté the mushrooms for about 3 to 4 minutes, until they are tender and appetizingly brown.

Stir the egg whites and parsley together. The egg whites should not get frothy, just mixed with the parsley. Very lightly grease an 8- or 9-inch nonstick frying pan with an oven-proof handle. Alternately, choose an oven-proof dish of comparable size. Pour in the egg-white mixture, and bake for 4 minutes.

Meanwhile, reheat the mushrooms. Remove the omelet from the oven, spoon most of the mushrooms and all the cheddar over half, and then fold the other half on top. Return to the oven for another minute. Slip from the pan to the plate, and garnish with the remaining mushrooms.

Serves 1

Breakfast in the Conservatory

These scones are wonderful for breakfast with Blantyre's marmalade and coffee, and just as good later in the day with a cup of tea. Oats are not traditional in English scones — that's why Christopher Brooks calls these "American" scones.

AMERICAN SCONES

2 cups all-purpose flour

1/2 cup rolled oats

2 teaspoons baking powder

1/2 teaspoon salt

1 stick cold butter

1/2 cup sugar

1/2 cup raisins

1/2 cup milk

1/3 cup sour cream

Preheat the oven to 400 degrees. Line a baking sheet with parchment paper or a silicone baking mat.

In a large bowl, mix the flour, oats, baking powder, and salt. Slice the butter into pea-size bits, and add to the flour mixture. Cut it in, or if using a food processor, whiz it until the mixture looks like coarse bread-crumbs. Mix in the sugar and raisins, make a well in the center, and add the milk and sour cream. Stir the dry mix into the liquids.

Using your fingers, pull the mixture together to form a dough. If it's too dry to do this, add a little more milk, 1 tablespoon at a time.

On a board, knead the dough just two or three times. Form into 8 scones, each 2 inches in diameter by about 1-inch high. (If you prefer small scones, form the mixture into 10 or 12 smaller pieces.) Place them on the cookie sheet quite close together — about 1 inch apart — because this helps them rise better. Bake for 20 minutes or until they've risen and are lightly golden.

Makes 8 to 12 scones, depending on size

BLUEBERRY MUFFINS

1 cup blueberries

4 cups all-purpose flour

3 teaspoons baking powder

1/2 teaspoon salt

1 3/4 sticks unsalted butter at room

   temperature

1 2/3 cups sugar plus 3 tablespoons

   for sprinkling on top

3 eggs

1 1/3 cups milk

Preheat the oven to 375 degrees, and line two muffin trays with paper cups.

In a small bowl, toss the blueberries with 1 teaspoon of the flour. In another bowl, mix the remaining flour, baking powder, and salt. Cream the butter and the 1 2/3 cups of sugar until pale and fluffy. Add the eggs one at a time and include 1 tablespoon of the flour mixture with each. Stir in the rest of the flour and then the milk. Finally, fold in the flour-dusted blueberries.

Fill the prepared muffin cups with the batter. Sprinkle the tops generously with the additional sugar, and bake for 20 minutes or until a toothpick or skewer poked into the middle comes out clean. Cool on a wire rack for a few minutes, and then serve warm.

These muffins freeze well. You can make a big batch and freeze half so you have enough for more than one occasion.

Makes 2 dozen

Blantyre serves these buttery, blueberry-dotted muffins year-round in its breakfast pastry baskets. The recipe is an old Fitzpatrick-family favorite.

It's worth having extra loaves of this versatile bread — it's good with soup or with cheese and terrific toasted at breakfast. This recipe makes a big batch. Freeze loaves you don't need immediately in a zip-top plastic bag. They defrost quickly and emerge as good as new.

DATE, ORANGE, *and* ROSEMARY BREAD

1 package active dry yeast
1 cup warm water or more as needed
4 cups bread flour
3 cups whole-wheat flour
1 teaspoon salt

1 12-ounce bottle IPA-style beer
Zest of 2 oranges
1 teaspoon rosemary leaves
2 cups (about an 8-ounce package)
chopped dates

In a small bowl, mix the yeast with 1/2 cup of the warm water, and let it stand until frothy. In a large warmed bowl or the bowl of an electric mixer, mix the bread flour, whole-wheat flour, and salt. Make a well in the center, and pour in the yeast mixture with the remaining warm water. Mix briefly; then add the beer, orange zest, and rosemary leaves. Using the dough hook of the electric mixer or your hands, mix and knead the batter, adding the date pieces a few at a time. If the dough is too stiff to mix, add more water, 1 tablespoon at a time, until it is easier to handle. When the dough is smooth and doesn't stick to your hands or the sides of the bowl, put it in a lightly greased bowl, cover with a large plastic bag or plastic wrap, and leave in a draft-free spot until it has doubled in bulk. It will take about 1 1/2 hours to do this, depending on the warmth and humidity of the room.

Grease loaf pans or baking sheet for rolls with oil. When the dough has risen, remove it from the bowl, and knead it firmly so it loses its bulk. Divide and shape into 4 or 5 baguettes or two large loaves in 9-inch by 5-inch loaf pans or 20 rolls. Cover the shaped loaves with plastic wrap, laying it on top but not tucking it in so the bread can rise. Put it in a draft-free spot to rise. When the loaves have doubled in bulk again — about 45 minutes — they're ready for baking.

Preheat the oven to 375 degrees. Rolls take 18 to 20 minutes, baguettes about 20 to 22 minutes, and large loaves about 35 minutes. Test for doneness by rapping the bottom: It sounds hollow when the bread is ready. Cool on a wire rack. If your loaves have been baked in a pan, let them stand in the pan for about 10 minutes before turning them out onto the rack.

Makes 4 to 5 baguettes, 2 large loaves, or 20 rolls

BERRY JAM

1 pound (about 1 quart) strawberries

1 pound (about 1 quart) raspberries

1 pound (about 3 cups) blueberries

1 pound (about 3 cups) blackberries

1 tablespoon finely chopped mint

1 vanilla pod

10 cups sugar

Put all the berries, the mint, the vanilla pod, and the sugar into a very large pan like a pasta pan, sprinkling the sugar all over the berries. Leave overnight.

Cook very slowly, uncovered, over low heat. Stir occasionally at first, more frequently as the mixture thickens. When it reaches a jammy consistency, it is ready. To make sure, test it by holding a large spoonful high above the pan and letting it pour back in. If the last few drops join up to make a mini-dollop, it will set. Remove the vanilla bean.

While the berries are cooking, sterilize jars with metal (not plastic) lids, such as 1-pint canning jars or recycled jars from store-bought jam. Sterilize the jars and lids by submerging them in a large pan of water and boiling them for 10 minutes. Remove from the heat, but leave them in the water until you are ready to use them.

When the jam is ready, dry the sterilized jars with a freshly laundered cloth or paper towel, and spoon in the jam, covering with a cloth to absorb any steam. Put on the lids when the jam is cold. Store in the fridge, and eat within 6 weeks.

Makes 4 to 5 pint jars

Chef de Cuisine Arnaud Cotar learned bread-baking from his father in France. Since coming to Blantyre he has been teaching his skills to other members of the culinary team, so that now most of Blantyre's toothsome breads, including all those served at dinner, are made in house.

Which is best on breakfast toast or muffins, Christopher Brooks's berry jam or his thick-cut marmalade? You can make both at home with this jam recipe and the marmalade recipe that follows.

The history of marmalade goes back to medieval Portugal, where it was made with quinces. But marmalade as we know it today is a British invention that is often traced back to an eighteenth-century Dundee woman, Janet Keillor. She was trying to find a use for Seville oranges, which are too bitter to eat raw. Her recipe was developed by her son, James Keillor, who opened a factory in Dundee. When Blantyre's builder, Robert Warden Paterson, was born in Dundee in 1838, the factory was already going strong — as it still is today. Virtually the entire Seville orange crop of Spain goes to Britain's many marmalade manufacturers, so Christopher Brooks's version replaces them with a mixture of regular oranges plus thickly cut ruby grapefruit, which gives the bitter edge that makes marmalade one of the great breakfast pleasures.

MARMALADE

2 large oranges (totaling about 2 1/2 pounds)
1 large ruby grapefruit (weighing about 1 1/4 pounds)

12 cups water
8 cups sugar, more or less as needed

Wash the oranges and grapefruit. Cut off the stubs at the stalk and blossom ends of the fruit. Halve the fruit, and squeeze each half into a sieve set over a large preserving pan or pasta pan to capture the juice. Discard the seeds from the sieve, but add any pulp to the pan. Slice each half in half again and then into pieces roughly 1 inch long and 3/4 inch wide. Try to keep the width the same for each piece so they cook at the same rate, but there's no need to be scrupulously exact about the length; pieces of differing lengths add interest to the texture of Blantyre's marmalade. Put all the fruit and peel into the pan and add the water. Soak overnight.

Cook at simmering point for about 1 to 2 hours or until the peel is very tender. To test, remove a piece from the pan, let it cool, and then rub it lightly between your thumb and forefinger. It should quickly disintegrate. If it doesn't, continue simmering until the peel reaches this stage.

Let the mixture cool down a little, and then measure it. For every 2 1/2 cups, add 2 cups of sugar, stirring it in with a wooden spoon over low heat until it has entirely dissolved. To check, tap the bottom of the pan with the spoon; if you feel a crunch, it comes from undissolved sugar, so stir some more.

Refrigerate a plate to use to test for setting. Bring the mixture to boiling point, and then boil as fast as possible, stirring more or less constantly to make sure it doesn't stick to the bottom of the pan. The marmalade will set after 10 to 20 minutes of boiling. To test if it's set, lift a spoonful a few inches above the pan, and let it pour back in. If the two or three final drops coalesce to form one large drop, setting point is near. To confirm, drop a spoonful on the chilled plate. Let it cool for a minute

then tip the plate. If the marmalade is only slightly runny and wrinkles when you push it gently with the spoon, it is ready. You can also test for setting with a candy thermometer: Marmalade sets at 222 degrees. Let cool for about 10 minutes, and then stir again to distribute the peel.

While the fruit is cooking, sterilize jars with metal (not plastic) lids, such as 1-pint canning jars or recycled jars from store-bought jam. Submerge the jars and lids in a large pan of water, and boil them for 10 minutes. Remove from the heat, but leave them in the water until you are ready to use them.

When the marmalade is ready, empty the water from the jars, and dry them with paper towel or a freshly laundered cloth towel. Fill the jars with marmalade to within 1/4 inch of the top, and then cover with a cloth to absorb any steam. When completely cool, dry the lids, and tighten them on the jars. Store in the fridge, and eat within 6 weeks.

Makes about 4 pints

A Note on Sources

As cited in the text, newspapers have been a vital source for the early history of Blantyre. In addition, many books have been consulted. Much information about the Berkshire cottages of the Gilded Age comes from *Houses of the Berkshires 1870–1930* by Richard S. Jackson and Cornelia Brooke Gilder (New York: Acanthus Press, 2006). Details of the Patersons' art collection derive from *Important Paintings . . . Property of the Estate of Marie Louise Paterson, Catalogue of Sale March 18 and March 19, 1938* (New York: Parke-Bernet Galleries, 1938). Hoagy B. Carmichael's *The Grand Cascapedia River: A History, Volume 1* (North Salem, NY: Anesha Publishing, 2006) provided information about Robert Warden Paterson's camp there, the quotation on page 30, and the photograph of Paterson on page 19. Richard Jay Hutto's *Their Gilded Cage: The Jekyll Island Club Members.* (Macon, GA: Henchard Press, 2006) describes the club and its members. Details about Andrew Carnegie and the quotations from Louise Carnegie on pages 31 and 33 come from Peter Krass's *Carnegie* (Hoboken, NJ: Wiley, 2002). Milton Rugoff's *The Gilded Age* (New York: Holt, 1989) is the source of much of the information about Paterson's era. Robert Warden Paterson's *Impressions of Many Lands*, from which the quotations in Chapter II are taken, was published in Boston by Henry S. Dunn in 1900. Copies are rare, and the book could not have been used here without the courtesy of the New York Public Library.

In addition, thanks go to Jennifer Atkinson, great-great granddaughter of Robert Warden Paterson and his second wife, Emma Downing Paterson, who provided the information about Paterson's parents, James and Ann, details of their life in Blantyre, Ontario, and family knowledge about Robert Warden Paterson's brothers. She also often pointed the way to Internet resources.

References librarians, especially Melinda McIntosh, at the W.E.B. Dubois Library of the University of Massachusetts, unearthed many details, and Mary Robertson of the Cascapedia Museum forwarded material about the Cascapedia River. Judith Barter of the Art Institute of Chicago made available the Parke-Bernet catalog noted above. Grateful thanks to them all.

Laurel Suite writing desk

Calla lilies in the Music Room,
one of the many rooms of Blantyre kept so perfectly by Perri and her housekeeping staff

Adam A	Bambi J	Chris K	Deana L	Humberto S	Juan I
Adam H	Barbara C	Christelle C	Debbie B	Ian F	Julia K
Alex V	Barbara M	Christina A	Deisiane T	Jason N	Kelly C
Andrew C	Beth S	Christine R	Diogo T	Jesi L	Lisa S
Angela R	Brian M	Colette L	Dorothee S	Joan B	Liz L
Anita R	Carol M	Connie L	Eileen S	Jodi B	Luc C
Ann B	Carol S	Cristina M	Gracie B	Jolene D	Lynne S
Annabel S	Cesar A	Dan H	Greg S	Jon M	Maria R
Arnaud C	Chris B	David O	Holger H	Jordan B	Marty S

Mary B	Paul P	Santa C	Tristan J	Erin M	Katie B
Mattie B	Perri S	Sara B	Viktor K	Frank S	Kelsey L
Megan R	Phil B	Sharon T	Warren M	Hannah D	Linda F
Mike S	Phillip T	Simon C		Ivon de S	Marcos G
Molly W	Robert C	Sonia V	*Not in the photo*	Ivone D	Maureen G
Nicole A	Ron J	Sonja H	Al D	Jenny M	Shaunna L
Pascal P	Ruby B	Sonja H	Betsy H	Joanie N	Suzanne R
Pat L	Ruth B	Spencer L	Carla R	Joni C	Theresa A
Paul H	Ruth G	Trish M	Doug S	Joy M	Wendy N

Table bouquets waiting to be brought upstairs to the Dining Room

List of Recipes

Photo Credits

Rick Bambery: 236

Scott Barrow: 91

David Dashiell: 16

Sean McLaughlin: 2, 5, 57, 84, 88, 94, 109, 114, 116, 120, 124, 127, 129, 130, 132, 134, 136, 137, 138, 140, 142, 146, 152, 159, 162, 167, 173, 174, 177, 178, 179, 180, 181, 184, 189, 193, 194, 195, 199, 200, 203, 204, 205, 209, 210, 217, 218, 220, 233, 234, 238

Karen Radkai: 86

James Ringrose: 87, 104, 106, 145, 149, 156, 164, 168, 182, 185, 192, 227, 231

George Ross: 4, 6, 8, 10, 45, 47, 59, 61, 62, 64, 65, 66, 67, 68, 69, 70, 71, 72, 74, 75, 77, 78, 80, 81, 82, 93 96, 97, 100, 101, 103, 119, 123, 126, 131, 141, 151, 155, 157, 158, 163, 169, 170, 171, 190, 196, 206, 208, 212, 214, 221, 223, 225, 240

Kevin Sprague: 166, 187

Colonial Homes (Feb1990): 58

Courtesy of Lenox Library: 17, 20, 23, 29, 31, 32, 33, 35, 36, 38, 40, 44, 46, 49, 51, 54

Printing and Engraving by Thornwillow
Press Ltd: 98

Wallpaper selections photographed by Sean McLaughlin: Schumacher 12–13 and 92–93, Cowton & Tout 22–23, Scalamandre 50–51, Pierre Deux 56–57, Brunschwig & Fils 232–233

Ice House Bedroom